Oxfo...

C000066688

Staging of English History

OXFORD SHAKESPEARE TOPICS
Published and Forthcoming Titles Include:

Oxford Shakespeare Topics

Shakespeare and the Staging of English History

JANETTE DILLON

OXFORD
UNIVERSITY PRESS

OXFORD
UNIVERSITY PRESS

Great Clarendon Street, Oxford OX2 6DP

Oxford University Press is a department of the University of Oxford.
It furthers the University's objective of excellence in research, scholarship,
and education by publishing worldwide in

Oxford New York

Auckland Cape Town Dar es Salaam Hong Kong Karachi
Kuala Lumpur Madrid Melbourne Mexico City Nairobi
New Delhi Shanghai Taipei Toronto

With offices in

Argentina Austria Brazil Chile Czech Republic France Greece
Guatemala Hungary Italy Japan Poland Portugal Singapore
South Korea Switzerland Thailand Turkey Ukraine Vietnam

Oxford is a registered trade mark of Oxford University Press
in the UK and in certain other countries

Published in the United States
by Oxford University Press Inc., New York

British Library Cataloguing in Publication Data
Data available

Library of Congress Cataloging in Publication Data
Library of Congress Control Number: 2011945234

Typeset by SPI Publisher Services, Pondicherry, India
Printed in Great Britain
on acid-free paper by
MPG Books Group, Bodmin and King's Lynn

ISBN 978–0–19–959316–3 (Hbk.)
ISBN 978–0–19–959315–6 (Pbk.)

1 3 5 7 9 10 8 6 4 2

Acknowledgements

My thanks go to Peter Holland and Stanley Wells for suggesting this book to me, for holding faith with it throughout, and for reading and commenting on the entire draft. Thanks too to Simon Shepherd for sharing ideas with me at a very early stage, and to Brean Hammond for reading and discussing ideas and drafts with me as the book progressed. I am grateful to the School of English at the University of Nottingham for giving me research leave to write the book; and grateful too to the staff at Oxford University Press who saw the book through the press: Jacqueline Baker, who commissioned it, Jackie Pritchard, who copy-edited it, Rosemary Roberts, who turned proof-reading into an art-form, and Brendan MacEvilly, who oversaw production.

Contents

All quotations from Shakespeare's history plays are taken from the separate Oxford editions of the plays (listed below), except in the case of *Richard II*, which has not yet appeared in the Oxford series. Quotations from *Richard II* and Shakespeare's other plays are taken from *William Shakespeare: The Complete Works*, ed. Stanley Wells and Gary Taylor, 2nd edn. (Oxford: Clarendon Press, 2005). Stage directions in the Oxford editions are often silently emended, so substantive differences between the edited versions and the early texts are mentioned either in the notes or in the text, and Chapter 9 cites all stage directions directly from the First Folio text.

All titles and quotations from early modern texts have been modernized.

King John, ed. A. R. Braunmuller (1989).
1 Henry IV, ed. David Bevington (1987).
2 Henry IV, ed. René Weis (1997).
Henry V, ed. Gary Taylor (1982).
1 Henry VI, ed. Michael Taylor (2003).
2 Henry VI, ed. Roger Warren (2003).
3 Henry VI, ed. Randall Martin (2001).
Richard III, ed. John Jowett (2000).
Henry VIII, ed. Jay L. Halio (1989).

1

Introduction

Dead March. Enter the funeral of King Henry the Fifth, attended on by the Duke of Bedford, Regent of France; the Duke of Gloucester, Protector; the Duke of Exeter; the Earl of Warwick; the Bishop of Winchester; and the Duke of Somerset; [Heralds].

This is the opening stage direction of *1 Henry VI*. It scripts a highly ceremonial entry, to solemn music.[1] The term 'funeral' signifies a coffin, probably borne on a wheeled chariot and richly adorned with cloth of gold and armorial emblems, and the mourners, who enter, dressed in black hooded mourning robes, in order of precedence (the Regent of France before the Protector of England, his younger brother, and both brothers of the dead Henry V before other mourners).[2] Their entry on to the stage is slow, stately, and indicative of the solemn significance of the death of a king; and it gradually fills the stage, bringing on six named characters and several heralds as well as the coffin itself, probably mounted on a wheeled hearse. Both the slow pace and the full stage contribute to the way the entrance creates a sense of ceremony and grandeur about the opening of this play.

This is a book that will encourage sustained attention to stage directions and stage pictures, which means that words like 'probably' will figure frequently, since we have limited evidence of the detail of early modern productions. Such evidence as we do have, however, including inventories of costumes and props and occasional eyewitness testimony, suggests that the players invested heavily in rich costumes and often had access to the clothes actually worn by the rich and powerful of Elizabethan society.[3] Indeed, as Thomas Platter noted in 1599:

it is the English usage for eminent lords or knights at their decease to bequeath and leave almost the best of their clothes to their serving men, which it is unseemly for the latter to wear, so that they offer them then for sale for a small sum to the actors.[4]

The likelihood, then, is that the funeral entry that opens *1 Henry VI* was costumed and enacted in a way that simulated actual royal funerals at the time of production (which, given the persistence of ceremonial traditions, were not vastly different from royal funerals in 1422, the date of Henry V's death).[5]

One of the few certainties about the earliest productions of the play in 1591–2, as Michael Taylor notes in his introduction to *1 Henry VI*, is their popularity.[6] Philip Henslowe's Diary records regular performances and high box-office receipts over that period, and Thomas Nashe famously described the huge emotional impact of Talbot, the warrior-hero of the play, on playhouse audiences:

How would it have joyed brave Talbot (the terror of the French) to think that after he had lain two hundred years in his tomb, he should triumph again on the stage, and have his bones new embalmed with the tears of ten thousand spectators at least (at several times) who in the tragedian that represents his person, imagine they behold him fresh bleeding.[7]

One of the many uncertainties, however, is whether Nashe himself had a hand in writing the play. He may even have written the opening scene that is at the centre of this chapter; but since Shakespeare's dramaturgy was often collaborative and must be understood within the context of influential predecessors like Kyd and Marlowe as well as his collaborators and other contemporaries, this need not be a reason for replacing this scene here with a scene of more certain authorship. Shakespeare's histories are explored in this book as the product of a whole emergent new theatre culture in newly built permanent playhouses, not as the output of a solitary genius.

In order to understand how they were conceived and scripted we have to know something about the structure and design of the early playhouses for which they were written. Indeed the primary emphasis of this book will be on how Shakespeare (and his collaborators, where relevant) wrote specifically for these stages, which had only been established in London since the building of the Theatre in 1576, a mere fifteen years or so before Shakespeare's first play for the London stage. (The Red Lion, built in 1567, pre-dated the Theatre as the first permanent professional playhouse in London, but evidence regarding its cost and design does not imply a structure of the grandeur and permanence of the Theatre and its successors.[8]) The Theatre, where several of Shakespeare's earliest plays were first performed, was a circular outdoor structure open to the sky. So too were the Rose, where *1 Henry VI* was performed by Lord Strange's Men in 1592–3; the Curtain, where the Lord Chamberlain's Men performed in 1597–9; and the Globe, where Shakespeare's plays were routinely performed from 1599 onwards.[9] The Rose, even after its enlargement in 1592, was smaller than the Globe, and possibly also than the Theatre, but all three of these playhouses shared the basic layout of a stage protruding into an open yard for standing spectators, with further spectators' galleries on three, or possibly four sides of the stage.[10] There was a tiring-house at the back of the stage with two or three doors in it for actors to make their entrances and exits and a gallery for musicians and any scenes that involved actors positioned 'above'.[11] The only contemporary illustration of an Elizabethan playhouse interior is the famous De Witt sketch of the Swan. Some of its detail is highly ambiguous, but its broad outline does indicate the basic actor–audience relationship of the Elizabethan stage, with the audience surrounding a thrust stage, some in very close proximity to the actors, and able to see one another as clearly as they could see the actors.[12]

The construction of permanent playhouses and the opportunity to design playhouse interiors were, as already indicated, new to England in the 1570s; but construction and design were naturally influenced by earlier performance practices. Medieval and Tudor performance took place in a very wide range of spaces, from open fields, streets, and market squares to great halls, churches, inns, and innyards, and most of these venues continued to be used well after the building of permanent playhouses, and of course outside London, where there were very few playhouses. This range of venues, and the essentially itinerant nature of much early performance, meant that plays had to be highly adaptable to different spaces; and one way of describing that adaptability is to think in terms of performance as a dialogue between two ways of using space. The terms usually used for this way of conceiving performance are 'place and scaffold' or (in Latin, and in reverse) 'locus and platea'. What they describe is a flexible practice that moves between defined locations that represent particular places (as, for example, a scaffold may stand for Jerusalem or Pilate's house) and undefined open space (where, for example, actors may speak directly to the audience or make topical reference to the real world they both inhabit). In a similar way, the Elizabethan playhouse stage can accommodate both designated locations and unlocatedness; it can fix the action in time and place or it can produce a fluidity that floats free of singular time or place. When a throne (or 'state', as it was more commonly known in Shakespeare's time) is pushed out on to the stage in *Hamlet* the audience recognizes that the location of the scene is a state room and that the occupant of the throne is the King or Queen; and when an actor begins to dig an imaginary grave and throw up skulls, they recognize that the location is a graveyard; but when the Gravedigger tells the disguised Hamlet that Hamlet has been sent to England because the people are all mad there, the audience fleetingly exchanges its sense that the scene is set in an imaginary Danish graveyard for an awareness of where they are here and now and a recognition that the playwright is giving the actor a joke which brackets the fiction off for a few moments.

The shared familiarity of early modern writers, players, and audiences with the flexible use of space that constitutes place-and-scaffold may be understood as a kind of common spatial code, a spatial practice that conveyed particular kinds of meaning and relationship in a way that was so strongly internalized as to be obvious at the time, but which nowadays has to be more explicitly demonstrated and explained to become accessible. This is true not only of spatial practice but of other aspects of performance, such as costume, props, gesture, and movement; and it is partly the aim of this book to make those practices evident and accessible through the analysis of multiple examples. The book also has the more specific aim, however, of identifying which particular aspects of performance practice are especially characteristic of Shakespeare's history plays. This is not to imply that they are characteristic only of Shakespeare or only of history plays. As indicated above, Shakespeare was a dramatist (and a practising actor) within the same context as his collaborators and colleagues in the theatre profession. Many of the forms that will be examined in this book will also be found in Shakespeare's other plays and in the work of other dramatists. Yet I hope it will become clear nevertheless that Shakespeare's English history plays are constructed out of particular scenic units (both whole scenes and shorter units of action) which are especially recurrent and familiar to the genre, and that looking closely at the nature and use of these scenic units can bring us closer to understanding what Shakespeare was trying to do with these plays in his own time.

Since the aim of the book is so strongly focused on the nature and meaning of performance on early modern stages, it will engage very little with later productions, which usually, and rightly, aim to design forms of staging that will bring out meanings of interest and relevance to later audiences. Some modern productions, of course, have used minimal or quasi-Elizabethan staging very productively, as for example did Katie Mitchell's production of *3 Henry VI* for the Royal Shakespeare Company in 1994:

[the production's] staging reduces the contest to its basic components and the kingdom to a plaything: an upstage door, a window for siege debates, a downstage throne. It is as diagrammatic as a board-game, with every fresh atrocity coming as casually as the throw of a dice.[13]

But the objective here is not to describe or evaluate recent productions. It is to recover what Alan Dessen calls 'a theatrical vocabulary accessible, even obvious, then [to Shakespeare, his fellow players and his playgoers] but easily blurred or eclipsed today'. Modern productions, as Dessen observes, 'rather than helping to bridge this gap in our understanding can instead widen it (so as to become part of the problem rather than part of the solution)'.[14] Repetitions and variations of particular stage images are crucial to Shakespeare's early history plays, and omitting or altering these for a modern audience can erase important patterns within a single play as well as its links with other plays in the same series.

Let us return, then, to the opening scene of *1 Henry VI* to look more closely at the kind of theatrical vocabulary it uses and how this vocabulary would have spoken to early modern audiences. Though it may well not be the first scene of a history play that Shakespeare ever wrote, it is the first scene of what is known as the First Tetralogy, i.e. the first set of four history plays structured in chronological sequence.[15] As such it sets out the situation from which this whole sequence begins. The play opens with a death; and the opening scene thus strikes the falling cadence that is to permeate the whole play. The high points for England in the Hundred Years War, the victory at Agincourt and the conquest of France, are already in the past when this play opens; and the sequence of the three parts of *Henry VI* is one leading downwards, through further losses in France and English civil war (the Wars of the Roses). Not until he came to write *Henry V* at the end of the decade would Shakespeare seek to dramatize the triumphs from which the *Henry VI* plays fall away so rapidly.[16] Here, in *1 Henry VI*, the scene opens with solemn music and a silent procession before setting the characters to speak in hierarchical order and high rhetoric. Bedford, as the eldest surviving brother of Henry V, is thus the first to speak, and his first words are a formal invocation of the extreme lamentation due to a king of this stature:

> Hung be the heavens with black! Yield day to night!
> Comets, importing change of times and states,
> Brandish your crystal tresses in the sky,
> And with them scourge the bad revolting stars
> That have consented unto Henry's death—
> King Henry the Fifth, too famous to live long.
> England ne'er lost a king of so much worth. (1–7)

Gloucester, the younger brother, echoes his praise, conjuring up a picture of the conquering Henry with 'arms spread wider than a dragon's wings' (11), and Exeter brings in a note of anger and defiance, at the same time making formal reference to the picture that they, the mourners, make on stage ('We mourn in black' (16); 'our stately presence' (21); 'Like captives bound to a triumphant car' (22)). Winchester, while endorsing the line of praise, speaks only briefly, and then to affirm the Church's role in Henry's success:

> The battles of the Lord of Hosts he fought;
> The church's prayers made him so prosperous. (31–2)

The entry of a procession by definition places the actors in a linear arrangement, but as they arrive on stage and the coffin comes to rest they must place themselves in some order around it. Stage directions in early modern plays almost never specify this kind of detail, and the blocking of such scenes would have emerged out of a combination of rehearsal, previous practice, and a deep sense of social order. With a schedule of performance that programmed a different play six afternoons a week, leaving very little time for rehearsal, actors must have relied heavily on instinct and repetition in how they stood and moved on the stage; and evidence from beyond the theatre suggests that early modern actors and audiences had a strong shared sense of 'right' and 'wrong' about position and movement in social space and were inured to the idea that spatial and kinetic practice encoded certain aspects of social relationship.[17] Space was categorized both vertically and horizontally not only in ceremonial practice but also to some degree in everyday life. From childhood onwards, for example, children learned to kneel to their fathers, and women learned to seat themselves on the left of men, in a social system where right took precedence over left. In positioning themselves around the coffin, therefore, the actors would have been prompted by their sense of what was proper on such an occasion to each character in terms of his rank and relationship to the deceased King.

The coffin (given its size, the central importance of the King whose funeral this is, and the centrality of the coffin to any funeral ceremony) would almost certainly be positioned centre stage; and the mourners probably divided themselves on either side of the coffin according to precedence, with the Duke of Bedford standing on the right of, and close to, the coffin at the front, the Duke of Gloucester standing left front, and the remaining mourners joining them on either side and behind, further away from the coffin. (The term 'front', it must be remembered, however, is being used here of a stage which does not have the audience positioned entirely in front of it, but around three and possibly four sides, depending on the playhouse. Different sections of the audience would find themselves in closest proximity and with the best sightlines to different characters on stage.) Alternatively, the mourners may have positioned themselves in kinship groups, with Henry's full brothers on the right and the descendants of the Beaufort side of the family, including the Duke of Exeter, the Bishop of Winchester, and the Duke of Somerset, on the left; or in alliance groups, which would shift Exeter to align himself with Bedford and Gloucester.[18]

However the actors were arranged, the point is that the arrangement would have been intended as meaningful and readable rather than random. The audience would have expected to be able to 'read' rank and relationship into the stage picture. Indeed it is often helpful to think of stage pictures as emblems or pageants, holding certain kinds of meaning still in visual and symbolic form, like the emblem books that were so well known in the period. Certain kinds of scenes, including those with a ceremonial shape, such as this funeral scene, are more likely to produce emblematic stage pictures; and when these orderly pictures break up into disarray, as they quickly do in this scene, that disorder is also readable in symbolic terms because of its disruption of expectation. As Bruce Smith has argued in a brilliant essay on the elements of pageant in Shakespeare's plays:

> pageant elements allowed Shakespeare to introduce into his early plays a second order of reality, 'higher' than the human intrigue—a plane of reality where thematic ideas stand forth in unforgettable definition and declare their meaning with unmistakable clarity.[19]

Thus, just as the initial stage picture of kinship groups surrounding the coffin is readable as an emblem of the orderly state marking and mourning the passing of its King, so the quarrel that erupts immediately following Winchester's hypocritical remark about the Church's prayers initiates a visible replacement of the celebratory, dignified, and respectful stances of mourning with the tense, antagonistic, and disrespectful stances of conflict, swiftly transforming the image of civic order into one of disorder, and setting up expectations of the civil war which is to follow in the play. Gloucester responds to Winchester's smooth self-congratulation with the accusation that his prayers were in fact directed to a more treacherous end, and the presence of rhyme makes this couplet stand out from the surrounding verse, marking it as it were in audible italics:

> The church? Where is it? Had not churchmen prayed,
> His thread of life had not so soon decayed. (33–4)

Rhyme is a feature that recurs several times over in this scene (at 87–8, 143–4, 155–6) and is also often used to mark the end of a scene. It is another way of arresting the audience's attention, focusing it, as visual symbolism does, on the implications of a particular moment for both the wider action and the thematic plane, or what Bruce Smith calls the 'higher' order of reality.

As Winchester and Gloucester degrade themselves, the occasion, and the dignity of the state with their insults, Bedford calls them to attention by pointing out their neglect of the requisite order of the funeral ceremony itself:

> Cease, cease these jars and rest your minds in peace;
> Let's to the altar. Heralds, wait on us. (44–5)

His reference to the altar also has the effect of foregrounding the location, which in turn underlines the disgracefulness of this behaviour. Henry V's funeral, like that of most English kings, took place in Westminster Abbey, one of the most formal and sacred spaces of the English state. To quarrel in such a place, and on such an occasion, is more ominous and disturbing than to quarrel in a less revered location. Bedford, registering the seriousness of its implications, formally invokes the spirit of the dead King to protect the kingdom from civil war, but is not allowed to finish his prayer. Even as he speaks a Messenger enters from France with tidings 'Of loss, of slaughter, of discomfiture' (59). His careful and deliberate listing of each town gives the audience time to dwell on the seriousness and wider implications of these losses:

> Guyenne, Compiègne, Rheims, Rouen, Orléans,
> Paris, Gisors, Poitiers, are all quite lost.[20] (60–1)

They are not, and cannot be, of course, related to the quarrel the audience has just witnessed; but the point of timing the Messenger's arrival to coincide with the quarrel is to highlight how abruptly the English state has sunk into internal discord with the death of the great Henry V, imagined victor over all this catalogue of towns. The message of loss is made to look like an ironic response and rebuke to the bickering of the English lords who cannot even mask their differences long enough to carry out the funeral rites for their dead King. Even the Messenger openly rebukes them and summons them to 'Awake, awake, English nobility' (78). Such an address from a mere messenger to the greatest lords in the English state is unrealistic, but its very improbability gives it more emphasis.

The message hits home: Exeter laments the loss in words but Bedford immediately begins to remove his 'disgraceful wailing robes' as he calls for his 'steelèd coat' (85–6), creating another emblematic or 'gestic' moment.[21] He barely has time to react, however, before a second messenger arrives with news that the Dauphin is crowned King of France and of the French towns and leaders flocking to join him against the English. And yet again, just as the English lords begin to respond to this news, a third messenger arrives to tell them that the great Talbot has been captured. The repetition of this scenic unit, showing a messenger entering with bad news and the English grief and remorse that follow, constitutes a highly patterned way of representing the scale of English losses in France and the extent to which the English are themselves to blame for it. As suggested above, the writing is concerned with emphasis, not realism. This formal repetition makes the point clearly, pictorially, and memorably.

The third messenger breaks the pattern of brief report and swift exit with a long rhetorical speech describing Talbot's capture in detail, culminating in a contemptuous account of how Talbot, fighting undaunted, was only taken because of cowardice on both sides: Sir John Fastolf, who should have relieved him, 'Cowardly fled, not having struck one stroke'; and 'a base Walloon' stabbed Talbot in the back (134–8). The three messengers are followed by another pattern of three: the departure, one by one, of Exeter, Bedford, and Gloucester. Such symmetry is characteristic of the dramaturgy of Shakespeare's early history plays. Like pageantry and repetition, symmetry acts to make patterns more visible and thus to emphasize the significance of the action.

Elizabethan playhouses had either two or three doors in the tiring-house wall, so the choice of which door to use is usually an important one. (De Witt's drawing of the Swan shows two doors, but some had three.[22]) Much has been written on how the doors may have been used and whether there was an accepted code of practice that helped the audience to understand which offstage space was implied when a particular door was used.[23] But whether or not the use of the doors was as specific as some scholars have argued, it is clear that it makes a difference whether actors exiting in swift sequence exit via the same door or another door. If they exit via the same door the message given is that they are going in the same direction or perhaps with the same purpose; so it is likely that Exeter, Bedford, and Gloucester exit via the same door, though all go to different places to set about the preparations for war and for the safety of the young Henry VI (who was only nine months old when Henry V died).

Their exit leaves Winchester to speak his hidden thoughts to the audience. He is not alone on stage, since Warwick, Somerset, and other attendants on the funeral, together with the coffin, are still present, but Winchester's speech is an aside aimed at showing the degree to which he stands apart from the three who have just departed, and he would literally move away from the other characters on stage, and closer to one section of the audience, to deliver these lines. Shakespeare's history plays (though not only his histories) will often show this pattern of leaving a character on stage at the end of a scene, either alone or speaking aside, to share his villainous plans with the audience. *Richard III*, by contrast, marks a new departure when it opens with such a soliloquy.

Winchester first voices his sense of isolation and powerlessness:

> Each hath his place and function to attend;
> I am left out; for me nothing remains; (173–4)

and quickly follows on with his plan to change all that by seizing power:

> But long I will not be Jack-out-of-office.
> The King from Eltham I intend to steal
> And sit at chiefest stern of public weal. (175–7)

The scene closes on this ominous rhyme, and it is likely that Winchester goes out at a different door from the remaining mourners and the coffin. If the mourners exited through the same door as Exeter, Bedford, and Gloucester, leaving Winchester as the only one to exit through a different door, this would visually highlight the degree to which his character and purpose are set apart from those who work for the good of the kingdom.

This close look at one scene brings out many of the features that will form the subjects of later chapters. Chapters 2 to 4 concentrate primarily on the stage, building from a 'single' picture or tableau and the use of 'presenters' or choric figures (Chapter 2), through a horizontally divided picture, emphasizing opposite sides of the stage (Chapter 3), to a vertically divided picture, using the raised space of the stage gallery in addition to the stage platform (Chapter 4).

Chapters 5 to 8 focus more on the body: on how bodies move, gesture, occupy space, and handle objects in particular kinds of scenes. Chapter 9 concludes by focusing on the highly developed use of one crucial stage property, the state, in Shakespeare's last history play, *Henry VIII* (or *All is True*, as it was known in its own time). The aim will be to break down scenes into shorter units so that the building blocks of Shakespeare's historical dramaturgy become visible. The scene just studied breaks down easily, as we have seen, into such units as the processional entry, the quarrel, the messages, the exits, and the closing soliloquy. This is not the only way of breaking it down, of course. One very useful way of breaking down scenes into smaller units is to use the entrances and exits as a formal set of divisions, and this can be very instructive.[24] But in this book I am looking more closely at repeated units of action or stage pictures, in order to identify how these recurrent units are used and brought together to create the ten history plays considered here, which have many similarities with each other, but also important differences. Shakespeare's dramaturgy changes as he moves from the early to the later history plays and finally returns to the history play after a gap of thirteen years to write *Henry VIII*.

Inevitably there is some overlap between chapters focused in this way. The elevated chair of state, for example, figures in the discussion of the vertical organization of stage picture (Chapter 4) and the discussion of symbolic props (Chapter 5) as well as in the extended analysis of *Henry VIII* (Chapter 9); and particular scenes may recur in different kinds of analysis. But I hope such overlap and recurrence may be useful in pointing up the plurality of approaches that illuminate the interpretation of any scenic unit and may also suggest to readers ways in which the whole range of approaches applied here may be applied more widely across the plays of Shakespeare and his contemporaries. Though the focus of this book is the specific and developing dramaturgy of Shakespeare's history plays, many of the practices it identifies are also to be found in other plays by other dramatists. It was in the context of such shared social and spatial assumptions and shared theatrical practice that Shakespeare's writing, both individual and collaborative, emerged.

Pageants and Presenters

Although many scenes in Shakespeare's plays are not very specifically located, location is occasionally very important for particular reasons.[1] In *2 Henry VI* there is a scene where the rebel Jack Cade, on the run and starving, enters a garden looking for something to eat. He is alone on stage, and the audience knows the location and the situation because Shakespeare embeds the information into the opening lines, which are a direct address to the audience, outlining Cade's reason for climbing over the wall into the garden. Within a few lines, however, the owner of the garden, Alexander Iden, enters, unaware of Cade's presence.[2] Iden has not appeared at all in the play before this point, and his entry marks a visible and audible shift in the scene, indeed in the play. Cade is ragged and dirty, having been hiding out in the woods for five days, whilst Iden is a gentleman squire, costumed accordingly; Cade here speaks prose (though elsewhere he occasionally speaks verse) whilst Iden speaks verse; and where Cade's words immerse the audience in the realistic immediacy of the fictional here and now, Iden's take them out of it into a different mode of perception. Here is the end of Cade's opening monologue, followed by Iden's first speech:

CADE I think this word 'sallet' was born to do me good; for many a time, but for a sallet, my brain-pan had been cleft with a brown bill; and many a time when I have been dry, and bravely marching, it hath served me instead of a quart pot to drink in; and now the word 'sallet' must serve me to feed on.[3]

> *Enter Alexander Iden*
> IDEN Lord, who would live turmoilèd in the court,
> And may enjoy such quiet walks as these?

> This small inheritance my father left me
> Contenteth me, and worth a monarchy.
> I seek not to wax great by others' waning,
> Or gather wealth I care not with what envy;
> Sufficeth that I have maintains my state,
> And sends the poor well pleasèd from my gate. (4.10.9–23)

Their speeches are worlds apart. Cade's rough and jokey prose is focused on his immediate and pressing need to eat the salad leaves growing in the garden, whereas Iden speaks rhetorically and reflectively of his way of life, making the garden signify (temporarily) as an emblem of the good life. It is as though a real man, forcing an entry into a real garden in a real world where hunger is the driving force of his existence, suddenly enters an allegorical world in which an allegorical guide-figure sets before him the idea, or idealized essence, of 'the garden'. It is perhaps no accident that the man who presents this pageant is called Iden, spelled 'Eden' in Holinshed, Shakespeare's chronicle source.[4] His very name suggests the degree to which he stands at this point outside the immediate moment of the imagined real world of the play, forcing that world to pause briefly while an idea is rhetorically 'frozen' for the audience to contemplate its didactic meaning. All gardens in western literature lead back to the image of the Garden of Eden; and the Garden of Eden is in turn linked with the classical Golden Age, when plants sprang forth freely from the ground without the need for labour. They represent a locus for what is best in human beings, a setting in which even fallen men can come closer to the good life, free from envy, ambition, and greed, and finding peace and contentment in quiet contemplation and willing hospitality; and they are also regularly used to represent the state or commonwealth, in order to measure how far it achieves or fails to achieve the ideal harmony and order that the garden recalls. As such, gardens were widely familiar in court and street pageantry, and educated or observant spectators would have been aware of their connotations.[5]

Shakespeare has already prepared the way for this image of Eden in the scene which introduces Cade for the first time, where his false boasts of aristocratic descent are punctured by Sir Humphrey Stafford:

CADE It is to you, good people, that I speak,
        Over whom, in time to come, I hope to reign,
        For I am rightful heir unto the crown.
STAFFORD Villain, thy father was a plasterer,
        And thou thyself a shearman, art thou not?
CADE And Adam was a gardener.[6] (4.2.120–5)

Here Cade's words point in two ways, acting on the one hand as a corrective to Stafford's implied contempt for Cade's low social status, and on the other as a rather cunning diversion from the just accusation that he is telling lies about his background and hence his supposed claim to the throne. But the point is briefly made for the audience that there was no social hierarchy in Eden. The first and only man was a gardener, and tending a garden is an ancient and noble occupation. That reminder is there partly so that it can resurface more fully in the later scene, 4.9, where the garden becomes the setting for this encounter between Cade, a visibly fallen man in a very fallen world, riven by civil war, and Iden/Eden, a man who, though he will come to participate more realistically and problematically in the world Cade occupies as he slays him and carries his head to the King, is at this point a speaking picture, the presenter of a pageant.

As Bruce Smith comments, 'To introduce a pageant into the middle of a play is to confront actors and audience alike with an aesthetic challenge'; and it is one that modern productions and audiences do not easily rise to, as it is so unfamiliar.[7] In modern performance it is all too easy to misread Iden within the terms of assumed realism and hence to dismiss his position as 'smug self-esteem' or 'bourgeois complacency'.[8] But these readings are based on the misguided assumption that Shakespeare's characters are continuously realistic and developing psychologies and that any one scene or part of a scene is to be viewed in the same way as any other. This is quite simply not the case; and one of the reasons for writing this book is to try to make clear how much our current assumptions about theatre differ from those in place in Shakespeare's time. As Mark Rose puts it, 'the presentation of character in Shakespeare is perhaps less like a modern film in which the figures are in constant motion than an album of snapshot stills to be contemplated in sequence'; and Shakespearian dramaturgy routinely shifts between different modes in different scenes.[9]

To make the point that the stretch of action we have been discussing is not a uniquely special case, but part of a dramatic mode that Shakespeare often uses to change the way the audience views the play, we may compare it with a similar stretch of action in another play, *Richard II*. Here again, as the Queen and two of her ladies enter, the scene pointedly establishes the location straight away with the Queen's opening question: 'What sport shall we devise here in this garden?' (3.4.1); and here again Shakespeare has already paved the way for thinking about the garden as an opportunity for essentializing and universalizing the discourse of the play in an earlier scene, when the dying John of Gaunt laments the ruination of:

> This royal throne of kings, this sceptred isle,
> This earth of majesty, this seat of Mars,
> This other Eden, demi-paradise. (2.1.40–2)

England, the 'other Eden', has in Gaunt's view been ruined by Richard II's 'rash, fierce blaze of riot' (33), his spoilt and vain pursuits, and the ease with which he has allowed himself to be led by flatterers.

As in *2 Henry VI*, the garden in Act 3, scene 4 of *Richard II* briefly functions as a realistic location in which the Queen looks for ways to drive away her sorrow, but within a few lines the entrance of a second group changes the perspective. A gardener and two servants come on stage, and immediately the prevalence of simile and the implication of a wider metaphor indicate that this is not primarily a speech about gardening, but about the condition of England:

> Go, bind thou up young dangling apricots,
> Which, like unruly children, make their sire
> Stoop with oppression of their prodigal weight.
> Give some supportance to the bending twigs.
> [*To Second Man*] Go thou, and, like an executioner,
> Cut off the heads of too fast-growing sprays
> That look too lofty in our commonwealth.
> All must be even in our government. (30–7)

Again, as in *2 Henry VI*, the gardeners are watched and overheard by another figure already on stage who has a vested interest in learning the lesson this pageant seeks to teach. The co-presence of figures who function as either presenters or viewers of a pageant, furthermore, positions the audience to recognize a moment towards which they must pay a different kind of attention, a moment that pauses the onward movement of the plot in order to make the audience reflect on the development and significance of the play up to that point.

Its effect is somewhat like that of a Greek chorus, punctuating the structure of the play to reflect and comment on its progress; and elsewhere such scenes or episodes of punctuation in Shakespeare are sometimes more choric and less pageant-like. They are often recognizable, however, by their extraneous nature (they are in excess of the strict needs of the plot); by the fact that they are Shakespeare's additions to the source material; and by their brevity.

A very short scene in *Richard III* in which a Scrivener (a scribe, particularly of legal documents—never seen again in the play) speaks of what he sees shows very clearly the kind of function such scenes have in history plays. Here is the whole scene:

> *Enter a Scrivener, with a paper in his hand*
> SCRIVENER Here is the indictment of the good Lord Hastings,
>   Which in a set hand fairly is engrossed,
>   That it may be this day read o'er in Paul's.
>   And mark how well the sequel hangs together.
>   Eleven hours I have spent to write it over,
>   For yesternight by Catesby was it brought me;
>   The precedent was full as long a-doing;
>   And yet within these five hours lived Lord Hastings,
>   Untainted, unexamined, free, at liberty.
>   Here's a good world the while! Why, who's so gross
>   That cannot see this palpable device?
>   Yet who's so bold, but says he sees it not?
>   Bad is the world, and all will come to naught,
>   When such bad dealing must be seen in thought.
>
> *Exit.* (3.6)

Because this scene is not allegorical, and because it focuses on a written document that the Scrivener literally holds in his hand, it is easy to see how directly it prompts an audience to consider the way history is constructed, itself a written narrative based on the evidence of precisely such further written documents as this. It is a scene often omitted in modern performance, thus underlining the point that such scenes do not fit easily within a conception of Shakespeare's plays as continuously realist in mode. The Scrivener is more function than character: that is to say, he is invented and embodied by an actor for this scene only for a particular purpose. It is not he, but what he has to say that matters; but giving him physical embodiment on the stage gives the audience a picture to hold in their minds of an ordinary man holding a paper, registering a moment of insight: he sees through Richard's deceits and says so.

The Scrivener's point is that he has spent the last eleven hours writing out an indictment of Lord Hastings (a document to be read out in public justification of his execution), yet Hastings was alive and well and not accused of any crime up to five hours ago; so the document was prepared in advance of even the accusation, far less any trial. The audience has already seen Hastings's severed head carried on stage in the previous scene, and the swiftness of Richard's decision to execute him in the scene before that:

> Thou art a traitor.
> *[He claps his fist on the table.*
> *Enter Catesby and soldiers]*
> Off with his head. Now by Saint Paul,
> I will not dine today, I swear,
> Until I see the same.[10] (3.4.80–3)

Richard has shared most of his crimes and deceits directly with the audience, so they know already that he routinely disposes, with no concern for justice, of those he does not trust; but what this scene does is make them pause to reflect on what ordinary people outside the court knew and thought. The Scrivener suggests that any fool can see through 'this palpable device', but that none dares say it aloud, and his closing rhyme moralizes such actions to draw the general conclusion about the world that England has become under Richard of Gloucester, soon to be crowned Richard III.

This scene is based on an episode in Sir Thomas More's *History of Richard III*, as recorded in Holinshed's *Chronicles*, where More cites a schoolmaster and a merchant exchanging words about the obvious fraudulence of the proclamation, produced a mere two hours after Hastings was beheaded and obviously the result of a much longer process than that time could have allowed:

So that upon the proclaiming thereof, one that was schoolmaster of Paul's of chance standing by, and comparing the shortness of the time with the length of the matter, said unto them that stood about him, 'Here is a gay goodly cast foul cast away for haste.' And a merchant answered him that it was written by prophecy.[11]

In changing this dialogue between a schoolmaster and a merchant into a monologue by a scrivener, whose business is writing, Shakespeare focuses more pointedly on the very matter of history and makes his audience consider it for what it is: an act of writing based mainly on the evidence of earlier writing.

As many early modern writers of history noted themselves, the usual practice of historiography at that time was to incorporate the writings of earlier historians wholesale and without question into the work in hand, just as Holinshed incorporated More's *History of Richard III*.[12] Samuel Daniel describes and justifies this kind of practice in the 'Epistle Dedicatory' to his history of *The Civil Wars between the Houses of Lancaster and York* (first published in 1595):

I have carefully followed that truth which is delivered in the history; without adding to, or subtracting from, the general received opinion of things as we find them in our common annals: holding it an impiety, to violate what public testimony we have, without more evident proof; or to introduce fictions of our own imagination, in things of this nature.[13]

In other words, the authority of earlier historians must hold sway unless there is new evidence to bring it into question. Anything else is fiction, derived from the author's 'own imagination'.

There is, however, a further context for this kind of thinking besides respect for earlier authorities. History was a notoriously sensitive form of writing in this period, a recognized cover for topical political writing. Elizabeth I famously recognized herself as Richard II in John Hayward's *Life and Reign of King Henry IIII*, and had Hayward imprisoned in the Tower, where he remained until after her death.[14] (Prior to this books offered for publication were normally approved by the Church, under the authority of the Bishop of London and the Archbishop of Canterbury. Plays were licensed for the stage by the Master of the Revels, but the publication of plays required further authorization by the Church up to 1606.[15]) As

Hayward himself wrote many years later, reporting a conversation with Prince Henry, the son of James I:

men might safely write of others in manner of a tale; but in manner of a history, safely they could not: because, albeit they should write of men long since dead, and whose posterity is clean worn out; yet some alive, finding themselves foul in those vices which they see observed, reproved, and condemned in others, their guiltiness maketh them apt to conceive, that, whatsoever the words are, the finger pointeth only at them.[16]

There was—and is—no such thing as a neutral history book. Historiography, the writing of history, always arises out of the mindset of particular individuals writing in particular contexts. Edward Hall, for example, was a Protestant lawyer loyal to Henry VIII, and the shape of his narrative, as its title (*The Union of the Two Noble and Illustrate Families of Lancaster and York*) makes clear, is to show England's history as a movement from division to union, and thereby to praise the Tudor dynasty. The chronicle, or annal, strictly speaking a year-by-year record of events without a joining narrative, is the closest written history can come to neutrality, but even chronicles reveal a degree of bias through what they select and omit.[17] History, even when its writers claim that they are merely following the authority of earlier writers, involves selection and omission and necessarily reflects the organizing sensibility producing it. It is also endlessly capable of interpretation, which makes it a very volatile and risky form of writing, and this is why the Elizabethan authorities kept such a close watch over it.

Whilst writing history was becoming more difficult and dangerous, dramatizing it was becoming more popular. Indeed the rise of the history play in the 1590s may have been partly a consequence of the close monitoring of written history by the government and its agents. In the playhouse there was more freedom at this point. Though plays also had to be licensed from 1581, by the Master of the Revels, it was self-evident that remaking history as living action, gesture, and dialogue necessarily involved an act of imagination, and only obviously inflammatory material (such as the dramatization of the May Day riots in the play of *Sir Thomas More*, in which Shakespeare had a hand) was likely to incur censorship. Plays therefore had more space to adopt a sceptical or questioning stance towards the material of the chronicles;

and Shakespeare regularly introduced such questioning into his history plays, first by his selection, arrangement, and omission of chronicle material, and secondly by his alterations to the chronicle material and his insertion of new material. We can see selection and emphasis pointing the material in certain ways in the garden scene in *2 Henry VI*; alteration highlighting certain aspects of the Scrivener scene in *Richard III*; and the insertion of a wholly fictional garden scene in *Richard II* mounting a critique of the King in that play.

Often too, the clue to the audience to look sceptically at the actions of kings and high-born lords is the presence on stage of low-born figures: artisans, gardeners, and scriveners. If most Tudor history is written from the top down, seeing history through the lens of kings and queens and their reigns (Hall's Chronicle, for example, is divided and numbered in sections each beginning with the accession of a new monarch), dramatized history can offer a different perspective by inserting scenes that look at the actions of the great through the eyes of men firmly anchored in the jobs they do, who see clearly the distortion and corruption of ambition, greed, and a life led within the factional confines of the court. Such figures can be very different from play to play, however, and the thrust of the critique is not always in one direction. Though the Scrivener in *Richard III* and the Gardener in *Richard II* see the faults of the King and the problems of the commonwealth following from bad rule, the shearman Cade in *2 Henry VI*, in revolt against his social superiors, is as corrupt and untrustworthy as they are, and it is the gentleman squire, Iden, who presents the critique of a life of envy and ambition.[18]

Henry VIII, Shakespeare's last history play, co-written with John Fletcher in 1612–13, long after the writing of the other history plays in the 1590s, presents an interesting case in that it provides a sequence of choric commentators, all of different social status—the Old Lady in 2.3 and 5.1, the Gentlemen in 2.1 and 4.1, and the Porter and his Man in 5.3—some of whom appear more than once in the play, and all of whom are additions to the play's chronicle sources.[19] The Old Lady, who appears to be a court lady-in-waiting, is slightly different in kind from the others, since she enters into direct dialogue with Anne Boleyn rather than commenting from the margins, as the others do. But her function is primarily to put forward a cynical view of the interactions of kings and queens (or, in the earlier scene, future queens who are at present scarcely more than 'queans' (whores; as implied at 2.3.92)). In 2.3 she mocks Anne's apparent surprise at being made Marchioness of Pembroke, hinting that Anne is already know-ingly embarking on the course of making herself Henry's Queen; and in 5.1 she delivers the unwelcome news that Anne's child is a girl and complains at being paid too little. In both scenes the clear implication is that everything has its price, whether it masquerades as love or thanks.

The Gentlemen function more clearly in the role of presenters, since they communicate the great ceremonies of the Tudor court to the audience with 'attitude'. In 2.1 they meet as the Second Gentle-man is on his way to Westminster Hall to hear sentence pronounced on the Duke of Buckingham, on trial for treason. The First Gentle-man's dry response, that 'All's now done but the ceremony | Of bringing back the prisoner' (4–5), pointedly places at a sceptical distance those great court pageants which punctuate the play, using the word 'ceremony' to imply 'mere' ceremony, and thereby to suggest that court ceremony is always a front to distract the people from the true import of the events thus ceremonialized. Several of Shake-speare's contemporaries show clear awareness of the potential for ceremony to be used as a way of keeping subjects in order. John Hayward, for example, expressed the view that 'in pompous ceremo-nies a secret of government doth much consist, for that the people are naturally both taken and held with exterior shows'.[20]

In the middle of their conversation the ceremony of the prisoner's return crosses the stage in silent solemnity, as the stage direction indicates:

Enter the Duke of Buckingham from his arraignment, tipstaves before him, the axe with the edge towards him, halberdiers on each side, accompanied with Sir Thomas Lovell, Sir Nicholas Vaux, Sir William Sands, and common people. (55)

The Gentlemen first consider how terrible this would be if Bucking-ham were indeed not guilty of treason (thereby also inviting the audience to consider this possibility), then continue their conversa-tion to discuss the 'buzzing of a separation | Between the King and Katherine' (148–9) and to voice suspicion of Cardinal Wolsey's possi-ble involvement and motive. At one level their conversation functions to relay important information to the audience; but it does more than that. The very fact that these are men of middling status passing on rumour and gossip and doubting the good governance of the state, together with the fact that the scene ends with the First Gentleman becoming uneasy with their openness ('We are too open here to argue this. | Let's think in private more' (168–9)), encourages an audience to speculate on how the machinations of the great impinge on the ordinary lives of those beneath them on the social scale.

The frequency with which the great ceremonies of the court are distanced in this play either by third-person report, or by being presented as dumbshow while spectators comment on them, is a measure of the degree to which Shakespeare and Fletcher invite the audience to observe them critically. As Gordon McMullan observes: 'we are put on our guard as we watch this play of ceremony and spectacle. Everything we see which at first appears impressive or convincing may well turn out to be a major disappointment.'[21] Nowhere is this clearer than when the two Gentlemen meet again, to watch the coronation procession of the new Queen Anne. This procession, described in an exceptionally full stage direction indicating the glamour and formal orderliness of the spectacle (4.1.36), moves silently across the stage, but its majesty is significantly qualified by the framing of the Gentlemen's commentary. Again, their commentary has an informative dimension, since they make clear for the audience who each participant is as they process slowly across the stage, but what begins as a commentary that seems entirely positive about the Queen, as an 'angel', having 'the sweetest face I ever looked on', quickly turns into the suggestion that the King's sexual desire is the real motive underlying his supposed conscience, in discarding his first Queen for this younger model:

> Our King has all the Indies in his arms,
> And more, and richer, when he strains that lady.
> I cannot blame his conscience.[22] (45–7)

When a third Gentleman joins them, coming from the coronation itself at Westminster Abbey, the discourse becomes even more pointedly fleshly and sexualized. He has been, he says:

> Among the crowd i'th'Abbey, where a finger
> Could not be wedged in more. I am stifled
> With the mere rankness of their joy. (58–60)

'Rankness', besides carrying the meaning of 'crowding' (*OED*, sense 9(a)), also implies in this context violence, excess, and the fetid smell of sweating bodies. 'Rank' could carry the archaic positive sense of 'impressive' or 'splendid' (*OED*, sense 3(a)), which leaves the Gentlemen's conversation, as usual, on the edge rather than unequivocally critical, but in this crowd, where 'Great-bellied women | That had not half a week to go . . . | . . . shake the press [crowd]' like battle-rams (78–80), the negative senses are surely more dominant. All this, furthermore, is developed from a description of the coronation in Holinshed which makes no reference to the crowd.[23]

The last of the choric scenes in this play, cut from modern performances more often than any other scene in the play, is another scene focusing on the crowd, this time via the vain attempts of the Porter and his Man to control the number of spectators seeking to force their way into the court to see the christening procession of the new Princess Elizabeth. It begins with a very topical rebuke that takes the audience out of the fictional world via a reference to the noise of the Paris Garden bull- and bear-baiting arena that they must sometimes have overheard in the open-air Globe, a short step away. The opening stage direction directs '*Noise and tumult within*', and the Porter threatens the imagined offstage crowd behind the great stage doors: 'You'll leave your noise anon, ye rascals. Do you take the court for Paris Garden?' (5.3.1–2).

Yet, despite the evident contempt of the Porter and his Man for the 'fry of fornication' (33) forcing its way in at the door, which positions the audience to sneer at the common spectators of court events (and hence perhaps reflect on their own position in the crowded playhouse?), the scene also more subtly complicates any feeling of respect or awe the audience might be tempted to feel for court spectacle itself. When the Porter's Man asks how he should be keeping a crowd of this size and force out, the Porter responds with uncompromising frankness:

What should you do, but knock 'em down by th'dozens? Is this Moorfields to muster in? Or have we some strange Indian with the great tool come to court, the women so besiege us? (30–3)

Thus the terms in which the Porter dismisses the unruly crowd he is trying to keep out indirectly besmirch the image of the spectacle he is supposedly protecting from their presence, by comparing it with popular and baser forms of display. The picture of women flocking to see 'some strange Indian with the great tool' is directly comparable with the sexualizing of the crowd at Westminster Abbey in the Third Gentleman's report, and some of the grossness of both rubs off on the court spectacle at the heart of the discourse. Whilst the Abbey spectators are not the crowned Queen, and the imaginary large-tooled Indian is not the christening procession, their discursive framing of these most sacred court ceremonies has the effect of making any easy or unthinking investment in the solemnity of such spectacles impossible for an audience.[24]

Gordon McMullan argues that the Gentlemen are not truly choric figures because they 'do not cut through the confusion of events, as a chorus ought to do, offering an anchor of objectivity'.[25] It is doubtful that the role of the Greek chorus was to be objective, so the fact that the Gentlemen are not may be beside the point; but it is certainly the case that, far from offering objective clarification, their presence more probably provokes than dispels confusion in the spectators. The point of adding this kind of scene is to complicate the chronicle narrative, to reverse the perspective of top-down history temporarily so that the shell of glamour and inevitability falls away from the doings of monarchs and aristocrats, allowing the spectators to consider history as a set of contingent circumstances that could have been different. This was one aspect of Shakespeare's dramaturgy that Brecht took from Elizabethan theatre: its ability to create a questioning stance towards history (how did it turn out like that? how might it have been different?) rather than an unquestioning acceptance of it as given.[26] What the presenters and commentators in the history plays do is offer an alternative, not an objective, perspective.

The most forceful and ebullient presenter of an alternative perspective in the history plays is Falstaff. Falstaff, central as he is to two plays (*1* and *2 Henry IV*), and an important absent presence in a third (*Henry V*), is not usually thought of as a choric figure, but his role is often to pause and reflect on the scene just past, and to open up a perspective that makes aristocratic attitudes, especially towards war, look like posturing. This process begins as the Percy rebellion starts to take hold in *1 Henry IV* and continues into *2 Henry IV*. It is first audible, as well as visible, in two sets of rhyming couplets at the end of 3.3 in *1 Henry IV*:

> PRINCE HENRY The land is burning. Percy stands on high,
>   And either we or they must lower lie.
> FALSTAFF Rare words, brave world! Hostess, my breakfast, come!
>   O, I could wish this tavern were my drum! (195–8)

Imminent war begins to turn the Prince away from his low-life pursuits to thoughts of victory and glory; but both war itself and the Prince's sudden shift into heroic mode have the opposite effect on Falstaff, who dismisses 'rare words' and a 'brave world' in favour of breakfast and more ale. From then on, as the Prince's role demands him to be viewed differently, as a serious warrior rather than an alehouse joker, Falstaff's own refusal to respond to the demands of war with anything more serious than a determination to avoid it, and to exploit its opportunities for extorting money, makes the martial earnestness of the Prince and others look intermittently somewhat pointless and ridiculous.

This puncturing perspective is most powerfully pointed in Falstaff's speech on honour, which meditates on the fact that honour is simply 'a word', a thing of air with no power to 'set a leg' or 'take away the grief of a wound'. He who has it, Falstaff wryly remarks, is very likely to be dead. It is, he concludes, 'a mere scutcheon' (*1 Henry IV*, 5.1.129–40). This conclusion is especially interesting in measuring the distance Shakespeare's dramaturgy has travelled between the *Henry VI* plays and these later plays. In the opening scene of *1 Henry VI* scutcheons, or heraldic shields painted with coats of arms, function as emblems of glory and of the honour due to the great Henry V whose coffin is embellished with such display; and the dramaturgy of those early plays is strongly focused on pictorial emblems that are readable to the audience as signs that function as synecdoches (parts for wholes, crowns for kings, and so on). But here in *1 Henry IV* signs no longer necessarily function in this straightforward way. A scutcheon is no longer readable as a simple sign for honour and/or lineage. Seen through a cynical presenter like Falstaff, it becomes *merely* a painted sign, and thus as emblematic of its own painted (and by implication empty) status as of any honour it might otherwise signify. (The substitution of a cushion for a crown in Act 2, scene 4 is a further dimension of this more sceptical dramaturgy that will be discussed in Chapter 5 below. So too will some of the parodic effects of juxtaposed signs in the *Henry VI* plays.)

The presence of the very live Falstaff, lying on the ground and playing dead as the Prince kills Hotspur, has a similar function. No sooner has the Prince taken an emotional farewell of the 'great heart' that was Hotspur, and, further, of the 'Poor Jack' whom he supposes dead beside him, than the same 'fat . . . deer' rises up, launches into a comic riff on the virtues of counterfeiting, and stabs the noble corpse of Hotspur with a new wound, intending to lay claim to having killed him himself (5.4.86, 102, 106). The comedy is very dark indeed and Falstaff's manhandling of the corpse, which only moments ago lay in the dignified stillness of death as the Prince covered Hotspur's face with his own colours, twists a moment of poignant mourning into a grotesque and uneasy pantomime.

Falstaff's role as a cynical chorus continues into *2 Henry IV*, where he not only remains a commentator on matters of war, but also becomes a kind of chorus to the chorus, as it were, since the new figures of Shallow and Silence become a further chorus to this play. They first appear just after Warwick has uttered a speech on time and history which is itself audibly choric:

> There is a history in all men's lives
> Figuring the natures of the times deceased;
> The which observed, a man may prophesy,
> With a near aim, of the main chance of things
> As yet not come to life, who in their seeds
> And weak beginnings lie entreasurèd. (3.1.79–84)

The present time, in other words, will always repeat the patterns of the past. The subsequent conversation, then, of the ageing Justices Shallow and Silence, with their reminiscences about a shared (and much embellished) past, peppered with references to the deaths of old friends, speaks emblematically to the audience of old age and false memory, besides the predictability of both life and death. It is again Falstaff's role to prick the rosy bubble of their reminiscences in his soliloquy at the end of the scene: 'Lord, Lord, how subject we old men are to this vice of lying!' (3.2.289–90). The effect is to make the whole play seem a pageant, a set of man-made shows covering up unpalatable truths.

The barb, however, points back towards Falstaff himself too, as the pronoun 'we' underlines. As the play approaches its close and Falstaff keeps telling himself new lies about his standing with the former Prince, now the new King, the harsh light he has turned on Shallow and Silence in this scene comes to rest on him, exposing the falseness of his hopes and the vanity of *all* old men. In the closing scene of the play, Falstaff is, like the Gentlemen later in *Henry VIII*, chorus to a piece of high spectacle, the King's coronation procession. He is on the margin, where he has in a sense always been in the new King's mind, even in the tavern, but he is expecting to move to the centre of government, by stepping into the role of Lord Chief Justice. He plans to 'leer upon' the King as he passes in procession, and eagerly instructs his friends to 'but mark the countenance that he will give me' (5.5.6–7); but it is not to be. Instead, as he calls out to Henry with embarrassingly personal tenderness, Henry turns to the man who is to remain Lord Chief Justice despite Falstaff's hopes and orders him to ensure that Falstaff never comes within ten miles of the court again. Falstaff loses even his choric role as well as the central role he never had, and his last words are an unfinished protest as he is taken off to the Fleet prison: 'My lord, my lord—' (5.5.91). The Epilogue, the last of the play's choruses, points the way forward to Falstaff's death in the next play, *Henry V*.

Stage Picture

The Horizontal Axis

The last chapter looked at scenes where the presence of a presenter made particular episodes especially readable as pageants or emblems; but in a sense all Tudor dramaturgy is inherently emblematic to a degree that is now unfamiliar. Occasional speeches underline the explicitness of the kind of acting familiar on Shakespeare's stage, as when Constance in *King John* addresses the silent Earl of Salisbury:

> What dost thou mean by shaking of thy head?
> Why dost thou look so sadly on my son?
> What means that hand upon that breast of thine?
> Why holds thine eye that lamentable rheum,
> Like a proud river peering o'er his bounds?
> Be these sad signs confirmers of thy words?[1] (3.1.19–24)

Conventional gestures or 'signs', passages such as this imply, were routinely expected and adopted to convey feeling. They were also used as ways of signposting and highlighting narrative action. Pulling on boots, for example, indicated the intention to set out on a journey; being carried on in a chair, perhaps also wearing a coif (a close-fitting cap), indicated sickness; and a woman with her hair loose about her shoulders was going mad.[2] Violent death was frequently signalled by the bringing on of a severed head, and the accession and deposition of kings was played out through the crucial props of crown and state. Film, by contrast, has encouraged later audiences to look even in the theatre for understated realism—the curl of a lip or the raising of an eyebrow—and to dismiss more heightened forms of theatrical expression as comic or 'melodramatic'. It may thus come as something of a shock to realize the extent to which Elizabethan actors and audiences expected the stage routinely to communicate through fairly emphatic visual signs.

This is a stagecraft where every gesture is a potential emblem. Thinking in emblems was an Elizabethan habit of mind, partly inherited from medieval allegorical thinking; but Elizabethan writing, both on and off the stage, was also shaped by the rhetorical emphasis of a humanist education. Tudor humanism, as Joel Altman and others have shown, set great store by balance, teaching students to argue both sides of any question and furnishing them with a set of linguistic tropes which frequently echoed that same privileging of symmetry.[3] Such thinking is, as Mark Rose has argued, spatially oriented: it assumes the presence of a centre and looks for proportion on either side of the centre, whether the thinking is focused on an abstraction or on a visual image. As Rose shows, 'there is a connection between the addiction to the allegorical tableau and the spatial conceptualizations of Renaissance logic'.[4]

It should thus come as no surprise to find that it is not just separate props and costumes that function as emblems on Shakespeare's stage, but the whole picture they create, the way they are disposed around a centre and in relation to one another. Even reported or imagined scenes carry this spatial awareness, as when Henry VI pictures Margaret and Warwick pursuing their separate suits with the King of France:

> She on his left side craving aid for Henry,
> He on his right asking a wife for Edward.
> She weeps and says her Henry is deposed,
> He smiles and says his Edward is installed. (*3 Henry VI*, 3.1.43–6)

The four lines, divided into two pairs of two, are as spatially patterned as the picture they report. Such spatial awareness is not merely a matter of literary and theatrical habits of thought; it is also deeply ingrained in medieval and early modern social practice. Left and right carried inherent significance, with right always taking precedence over left.[5] It is thus not coincidental that Margaret is imagined on the left of the French King. She may be a queen, but she is also a woman; and a woman's place, as already noted in Chapter 1 above, was normally left rather than right of centre. At court, and in stage representations of the court, the centre would usually be the state (the throne). To position a state anywhere other than centrally would in itself be to encode an important message about where power resided. The disposition of others around the state was then readable as indicative of their status in relation both to the monarch and to the others on stage.

The design of Elizabethan playhouses, like the writing habits of their dramatists, encouraged attention to symmetry and balance in the blocking of scenes. Whether circular or rectangular, all the purpose-built stages that we know anything about in the period were thrust stages with rear walls (though stage-shapes varied and some had a much deeper thrust than others). As discussed in Chapter 1, entrance to and exit from the stage was through either two or three doors in the rear wall, and large props would also have to be brought on through these same doors. In theatres with three doors it is likely that the throne would be carried through the central door and placed either directly in front of it or further out into the centre of the stage. When the central opening was used as a discovery space (not a very frequent occurrence in history plays, where this kind of effect is rarely required)[6] that too provided a pivotal centrepiece around which other elements were disposed according to convention; and the shortness of rehearsal time would mean that actors relied heavily on existing theatrical and social conventions of spatial arrangement to block scenes, symmetry being one such convention and social hierarchy another. The presence of a gallery in the tiring-house wall and a trapdoor in the main stage also allowed for the possibility of vertical division of the stage, which will be the subject of the next chapter; but this chapter will pay particular attention to horizontal symmetry and its functions.

A classic instance of the way spatial, bodily, and verbal symmetry work together may be found in Act 2, scene 5 of *3 Henry VI*, a scene not found in the chronicle sources, but invented for the stage.[7] Here the horror and misery of civil war are demonstrated in patterned, rhetorical form; and this is a scene which also functions as a pageant (the kind of scene examined in Chapter 2 above), held still for contemplation and seen through Henry VI, who functions partly as a presenter for this scene only. Henry first appears alone, in soliloquy, taking time out of the battle to sit down on a molehill (almost certainly centre stage) and contemplate the 'grief and woe' (20) he sees around him.[8] His speech on the happy life of the shepherd is comparable with Alexander Iden's speech on the happy life (discussed in Chapter 2 above); but the difference is that Iden is living that life, whilst Henry can only imagine it. This momentary quiet is interrupted by an alarum (a call to battle, sounded on a trumpet or other instrument) and a double entry at two doors: *'Enter a Son that hath killed his father at one door with his father's body, and a Father that hath killed his son at another door, bearing his son's body'*[9] (54). The Son speaks first, as he enters looking to plunder the soldier he has just slain, but his words turn to tears as he realizes that the man he has killed is his own father. Henry, the still and central point on the stage, comments on the 'bloody times' (73) they live in and, unobserved by the Son, weeps with him. Then, with chronological as well as spatial symmetry (that is, following either side of Henry's speech as well as entering either side of him physically on the stage), a Father bearing a body that he also intends to pillage finds it to be his son and pours forth his grief. Henry again picks up and presents the Father's grief to the audience almost as an aesthetic object, one that echoes the symmetry of civil war itself in pageant form, as embodied in the red and white roses of Lancaster and York:

> The red rose and the white are on his face,
> The fatal colours of our striving houses. (97–8)

From here the verse proceeds in units of three, with Son, Father, and Henry speaking units of the same length in the same repeated sequence and with parallel content, so that as the Son imagines his mother's grief, the Father imagines his wife's. Their exits are physically parallel, as each picks up the beloved body and leaves the stage with it in his arms. The King remains seated throughout, an image of grief like 'Patience on a monument' (*Twelfth Night*, 2.4.114), as the Father and Son come and go, representing all the other fathers and sons who will undergo the particular grief of civil war. The symmetry of this scene works to intensify and to universalize the pain it shows. It becomes a sculpted and balanced image of grief to carry away and return to in the mind, almost like an aesthetic object focusing grief, such as a funerary urn or a gravestone.

Such scenes can also function to highlight antithesis, however, so that the difference, rather than the similarity, between the image on either side of the stage is what is illuminated. This is the case with the scene in *1 Henry VI* where the Yorkists and Lancastrians take the white and red roses for their emblems (a scene additional to the source material). Again, as in two of the scenes discussed in Chapter 2, the location is a garden, which functions emblematically, as an image of the commonwealth, as well as literally (since the opponents will pluck two roses). This time the stage direction does not script the two parties (who have left the Temple Hall quarrelling) to enter the stage through two doors, and they probably do not, since they are both coming from the same place and are already in dialogue; but it is likely that they quickly begin to group themselves on two sides of the stage, according to their loyalties, as the positioning of the two rose-bushes invites them to do. Richard Plantagenet, who plucks the first rose, the white rose that will become the emblem of the House of York, invites anyone who believes the truth to be on his side (and the scene never tells us what the quarrel is about) to 'pluck a white rose with me' from the same briar (2.4.30). Somerset follows suit with his parallel invitation to those who wish to support him to 'Pluck a red rose from off this thorn with me' (33). As each of the others on stage aligns himself with Plantagenet or Somerset, two opposing groups form (repetitions of the word 'side' in the speeches have physical as well as figurative force here), and the dialogue begins to pick up the same stichomythic symmetry as the civil war scene:

> RICHARD PLANTAGENET Hath not thy rose a canker, Somerset?
> SOMERSET Hath not thy rose a thorn, Plantagenet? (68–9)

The schematic opposition of this scene again provides in pageant form the basis for the next two plays, as they play out the Wars of the Roses.[10] Indeed it may be that in court scenes throughout the *Henry VI* plays from this point on the supporters of York and Lancaster routinely identify themselves to the audience as such by wearing white or red roses in their hats.

The climactic version of this kind of horizontally oppositional scene is the one that takes place on the eve of the battle of Bosworth at the close of *Richard III*, the final encounter in the Wars of the Roses, which will clear the way for the union of the two houses through Henry VII (a Lancastrian) and his marriage to Elizabeth of York. Again this scene (5.4) is Shakespeare's addition to his chronicle sources and does not figure either in the earlier play of *The True Tragedy of Richard III* (a Queen's Men's play pre-dating Shakespeare's *Richard III*, not to be confused with *The True Tragedy of Richard Duke of York*; see Chapter 1 n. 15 above). In Hall, Richard has 'a dreadful and a terrible dream, for it seemed to him being asleep that he saw diverse images like terrible devils which pulled and haled him, not suffering him to take any quiet or rest'; and *The True Tragedy* also has Richard report this episode as a dream.[11] Shakespeare further distorts and embellishes history in order to make the final battle take place on All Souls' Day (2 November), and hence the eve of battle on All Souls' Eve (or All Saints' Day), a suitable date for the procession of souls that appears to Richard and Richmond before justice is finally done.[12]

In the scene of the ghostly procession the two factions occupy separate sides of the stage, and the tents of their encampments divide them off from each other, allowing the focus of the scene to move from side to side, 'bracketing' one alternately from the other.[13] The tents may be curtained scaffolds, either free-standing or projecting from the tiring-house wall; they may be created through a combination of the open stage doors and the imagination; or they may be wholly imaginary.[14] Either way, the positioning of Richard and Richmond on the two sides of the stage confirms the imagined distance between the two camps and the oppositional placing of the two figures, who have by now become respectively demonized and idealized as villain and hero.

The scene parallels various actions and speeches in order to highlight the opposition between the two sides of the stage; and it is reminiscent both of the old morality drama, which placed an Everyman-figure between good and evil angels fighting for his soul, and of the closing scenes of the old mystery cycles, Doomsday scenes in which God sat in judgment, centrally positioned, dividing the souls of the dead into the saved, on his right, and the damned, on his left. Marlowe's *Dr Faustus* also retained this divided stage very prominently in scenes positioning Faustus between the Good and the Bad Angel urging him in opposite directions, so it was familiar to Shakespeare's audience not only from fading memories of mystery cycles they might have seen, but from the current popular stage, possibly even the same playhouse.[15] Barbara Hodgdon has argued persuasively that 'Shakespeare's secular history plays are strikingly innovative but not radically discontinuous with the only other dramatizations of human history he could have known—the mystery plays', but that when he borrows from them, it is 'always with the effect of analyzing the political process empirically rather than identifying the hand of God in the government of humankind'.[16] *Pace* Hodgdon, however, there does seem in this scene to be a marked emphasis on the hand of God.

The central space between the two opposing camps is repeatedly filled and vacated by a sequence of the ghosts of those whom Richard has murdered. The scene is a long one, and the rhythmic entrance and exit of the ghosts is performed eight times in all, with eleven ghosts, some grouped together in a single entry. Prior to the entry of the ghosts, Richard and Richmond settle themselves in their tents, call for ink and paper to plan the battle, issue questions and commands to their men, and finally sleep. Within these parallel actions, however, important differences separate them. Richmond is depicted as more nervous: his questions and commands come thicker and faster, his tone is less peremptory and his manner more affectionate towards his men. Above all, he differentiates himself from Richard by praying, and would almost certainly kneel to do so on Shakespeare's stage. Thus, while Richard's last words before sleep are anxious and edgy, working against the rhythm of the blank verse lines:

> Bid my guard watch. Leave me.
> About the mid of night come to my tent,
> Ratcliffe, and help to arm me. Leave me, I say; (55–7)

Richmond's, ending a long and rhythmic speech of prayer rather than a sequence of short utterances, are calm and controlled, putting himself in God's hand rather than that of his guard:

> To thee I do commend my watchful soul
> Ere I let fall the windows of mine eyes.
> Sleeping and waking, O defend me still! (94–6)

The sequence of ghost entries then begins with the entrance of the Ghost of Prince Edward. The symmetries are carefully constructed both within each ghost's speech and across the speeches of the ghosts, with some important variations. Each turns in sequence first to Richard, then to Richmond. The Ghost of Prince Edward speaks three lines to each, wishing death and despair on Richard and victory and the kingdom on Richmond, setting the pattern for those that follow. Particular phrases resound through the words of ghost after ghost, above all the injunction to Richard to 'Despair and die' (99, 105, 106, 119, 122, etc.). That injunction is partly balanced by the repeated phrase in the ghosts' address to Richmond: 'Live and flourish' (109, 117, 131–2), but the terms used to Henry are variations on a positive theme, with less deadly repetition. Buckingham, the last ghost, spells out the link with the old dramaturgy of morality plays by ending with this clear affirmation:

> God and good angels fight on Richmond's side,
> And Richard falls in height of all his pride. (154–5)

The outcome of the forthcoming battle could not be clearer, as confirmed through the contrast between the massively disrupted rhythms of Richard's mounting fear and self-division:

> Cold fearful drops stand on my trembling flesh.
> What do I fear? Myself? There's none else by.
> Richard loves Richard; that is, I am I.
> Is there a murderer here? No.—Yes, I am. (160–3)

and Richmond's smooth report of 'The sweetest sleep and fairest-boding dreams | That ever entered in a drowsy head' (206–7).[17]

The battle sequence that follows, formally initiated by the orations each makes to his men, continues to develop the symmetry intrinsic to the horizontal division of the stage.[18] The logical conclusion can only be a coming together of the two opponents in hand-to-hand fighting, which is what happens in the violent dumbshow of battle at 5.7.0:

Alarum. Enter Richard and Richmond, [meeting]. They fight. Richard is slain.

The action that follows, Stanley's setting of the crown on Richmond's head, echoes and redeems the fake show Richard has devised in Act 3 when he sets up Buckingham and the Mayor of London to insist on having him crowned whilst seeming unwilling to submit to their entreaties. That is another horizontally devised scene, but with Richard at its centre, when he appears in the gallery space '*between two bishops, aloft'* (3.7.89). His removal from the centre to one side, and from there to death, is the story of the second half of the play.

Horizontal division of the stage can also be used with irony, as is the case in *1 Henry IV*, 5.4, briefly discussed in Chapter 2 above. This scene has first shown three units of action which probably all move about the whole stage in turn: Douglas fighting the King; the Prince fighting Douglas to protect his father; and the Prince fighting Hotspur. But the stage direction following line 74 interrupts the fighting of Hal and Hotspur with the re-entry of Douglas and a parallel fight:

Re-enter Douglas; he fights with Falstaff, who falls down as if he were dead; Douglas withdraws. Hotspur is wounded, and falls.

As this direction indicates, two fights are now taking place simultaneously, either side of the stage. On one side the chivalric duel of honour that the play has seemed to set up from the start, between the King's real son and the son he wishes he might have had ('O that it could be proved | That some night-tripping fairy had exchanged | In cradle-clothes our children where they lay, | And called mine Percy, his Plantagenet!' (1.1.85–8)), is played out to the death, whilst on the other, necessarily seeming to comment on it, the fight between Douglas and Falstaff quickly turns to parody as Falstaff plays dead. Not only does one fight set the other in an ironic light, then, but so too does the fake death frame the true death in a way that renders its value questionable. Hotspur's valiant death in the chivalric and somewhat archaic mode of hand-to-hand combat is only briefly acknowledged by Hal's tribute to his honour and removal of his 'favours' (his colours) to cover Hotspur's mangled face.[19] When Hal turns to the other body lying and, with due qualification for the lesser loss of this friend, makes explicit the parallel between the two bodies ('Till then, in blood by noble Percy lie' (109)), that parallel immediately turns to parody as Hal leaves and Falstaff rises. His speech about the value of counterfeiting directly calls into question the life and death of a man such as Hotspur, for whom honour has been the only touchstone.

In an earlier scene in the same play, however, one focusing on private rather than public life, it was Hotspur who occupied the parodic half of the stage. This scene, 3.1, opens with Hotspur's explicit and intentional mockery of Owen Glendower and his claims to extraordinary spiritual powers, so it has already set up a crowd-pleasing opposition (for an English audience) between inflated Welsh rhetoric and English common sense. (This opposition between rhetorical flourish, often implying some degree of falsification, and plain speaking is one Shakespeare returns to throughout the history plays, from the opposition between the plain-speaking Humphrey, Duke of Gloucester, and his oily-tongued enemies in *2 Henry VI* to the opposition between the plain-speaking Henry V and the unreliable or more guarded French in *Henry V.*) Hotspur, Glendower, and Worcester discuss how they will divide up the country between them if their rebellion succeeds; and the scene shifts into a new mode as two women enter: Lady Mortimer, daughter to Glendower and wife to the English Edmund Mortimer, Earl of March; and Lady Percy, Hotspur's wife and Mortimer's sister. The women are there to take their leave of their husbands before they go to war; but Lady Mortimer speaks no English. She speaks repeatedly in Welsh, with Glendower translating for Mortimer, but as she seeks to express herself in non-verbal ways the scene divides into two parallel halves. On one side, Mortimer lies with his head in his wife's lap while she sings to him in Welsh; and on the other side Hotspur parodies their love-play by exposing its sexual innuendo: 'Come, Kate, thou art perfect in lying down; | Come, quick, quick, that I may lay my head in thy lap' (222–3). The music plays and Lady Mortimer sings throughout most of the rest of the scene, while her husband listens silently and Hotspur and Kate display a very different kind of interaction out of earshot on the other side of the stage:

> KATE   Lie still, ye thief, and hear the lady sing in Welsh.
> HOTSPUR   I had rather hear Lady, my brach, howl in Irish.
> KATE   Wouldst thou have thy head broken? (230–2)

Though this scene is so domestic, its division of the stage works very similarly to the division in 5.4 discussed above. On one side of the stage is a rather literary and archaic mode of action (chivalry in 5.4, romance in 3.1) and on the other is a more pragmatic and cynical mode of behaviour that frames its counterpart to look rather manufactured or 'performed'.

The horizontal division of the stage is thus a practice that carries over from the First into the Second Tetralogy of history plays, but its use is changed. Where in the earlier plays it is likely to function as a way of highlighting balance and symmetry, and thus as a way of framing the whole stage as a carefully composed and unitary picture, it becomes in the later plays a way of creating two separate pictures that offer competing perspectives. The questioning of history and of how audiences should see and judge it becomes more emphatic as Shakespeare continues the project of shaping history for the stage. A questioning set towards history is evident from the start of the project in the way sources are selected and characters are depicted, but this particular way of using the stage develops from being a tool that frames contemplative or emblematic moments to becoming one that explicitly puts a divided perspective on show.

Stage Picture

The Vertical Axis

Spatial awareness, within the inherently hierarchical nature of early modern society, was as strongly expressed through vertical stratification as it was through horizontal positioning. Indeed this aspect of spatial awareness has a much stronger residual presence in our own society than does its horizontal equivalent. We still expect speakers to be raised on platforms, preachers to be elevated in pulpits, and the 'top' table (defined horizontally) often also to be raised on a dais. Chairs of state on the Elizabethan stage, similarly, were not just centrally positioned on the horizontal axis, at the 'upper' end of the room; they were also raised on a 'halpace' or low dais. The term 'ascend', routinely used to signal taking possession of the throne, applied quite literally.[1] The monarch physically climbed up the steps to take his or her seat on the state.

3 Henry VI uses this image of ascent repeatedly to parallel and contrast the different claims of Henry VI and Richard Plantagenet, Duke of York, to the English throne. Act 1, scene 1 is set in the immediate aftermath of the battle of Northampton, as the opening line makes clear:

WARWICK I wonder how the King escaped our hands?[2]

As the dialogue later reveals, the location is the parliament chamber, and the scene is strongly focused on emblematic props and gestic moments that speak clearly and powerfully to the audience of actions and events. Richard, son of Richard, Duke of York, throws down the head of the Duke of Somerset in evidence of his achievements in battle; and within a few lines of this iconic gestus Warwick first anticipates, then requires, the enactment of a second gestus:

> Before I see thee seated in that throne
> Which now the house of Lancaster usurps,
> I vow by heaven these eyes shall never close.
> This is the palace of the fearful King
> And this the regal seat: possess it York,
> For this is thine, and not King Henry's heirs'. (22–7)

This is a solemn moment, demanding a very significant action; the ascent of the throne should not happen quickly or casually. York and his supporters prepare for it over several lines, carefully reiterating in words their place and position, both literal and figurative, and avowing the seriousness of their intent. The anticipation climaxes in this exchange between York and Warwick before York finally ascends the throne:

> YORK I mean to take possession of my right.
> WARWICK Neither the King, nor he that loves him best,
>   The proudest he that holds up Lancaster,
>   Dares stir a wing if Warwick shake his bells.
>   I'll plant Plantagenet, root him up who dares.
>   Resolve thee, Richard, claim the English crown. (44–9)

This is the cue for Henry VI and his supporters to enter, and York's act of hubris in usurping the chair of state prompts outrage amongst them.[3] The sense they have that this way of occupying space represents the state disordered and the world upside down is evident in the repeated vocabulary of ascent and descent, underpinned by an almost overwhelming sense of rightful place, reverberating through the dialogue:

> WESTMORLAND   Let's pluck him down.
>   My heart for anger burns, I cannot brook it.
>   . . .
> HENRY Thou factious Duke of York, descend my throne
>   And kneel for grace and mercy at my feet
>   . . .
> EXETER For shame come down
>   . . .
> HENRY And shall I stand, and thou sit in my throne? (59–85)

York remains seated on the raised throne while the argument proceeds about whose claim is the more just. Henry himself admits in an aside that his claim is weak, and the Duke of Exeter shifts allegiance from Henry, persuaded by York's claim. Another physical sign signals York's growing power, as Warwick stamps his foot to summon his soldiers and so demonstrate the military backing of the Yorkist party:

> Do right unto this princely Duke of York
> Or I will fill the house with armèd men,
> And o'er the chair of state where now he sits,
> Write up his title with usurping blood.
>   *He stamps with his foot, and the Soldiers show themselves.* (167–70)

Not until a deal is struck in York's favour, that Henry may reign for the duration of his own lifetime but will entail the crown to York and his heirs upon his death, do York and his followers descend ceremonially, while a sennet sounds.

The image of the elevated monarch, however, continues to structure the play with pointed irony, since such a resolution can in truth satisfy neither side. Henry's wife and son express their rage as soon as they hear of this settlement, and by Act 1, scene 2, York's sons are already persuading their father that he must make good his claim to the kingdom through open war. Within short space York is surrounded by Lancastrians on the field of battle. Clifford has his sword drawn ready to kill York, but Margaret stops him in order to ensure that York suffers torment. The punishment must take place in an elevated place that echoes the dais (and may even be represented by the same stage prop) so that its poetic justice is clear:

> MARGARET Come make him stand upon this molehill here,
>   That raught at mountains with outstretchèd arms
>   Yet parted but the shadow with his hand. (1.4.67–9)

Margaret even crowns him with a paper crown, and orders her lords to bow low to him as she sets it upon his head, reminding them that 'this is he that took King Henry's chair' (97). The scene resembles those scenes in the mystery cycles where Christ is taunted and tormented prior to his crucifixion, as well as his crowning with thorns.[4] Holinshed also draws the parallel with the mockery of Christ:

Some write that the duke was taken alive, and in derision caused to stand upon a molehill, on whose head they put a garland instead of a crown, which they had fashioned and made of sedges or bulrushes; and having so crowned him with that garland, they kneeled down afore him (as the Jews did unto Christ) in scorn, saying to him; Hail king without rule, hail king without heritage, hail duke and prince without people or possessions.[5]

The molehill returns, as we saw in Chapter 3 above, in a later battle. Henry explicitly selects 'this molehill' at the battle of Towton (2.5.14) as a place to sit, which should again remind the audience of York's molehill and the dais, even if they are not all placed in exactly the same location on the stage (as they may well have been). His static, contemplative posture on the molehill contrasts with both of York's postures (his imperious occupation of Henry's throne and the shaming and pitiable reversal of this hubris as he is mocked by his enemies). The passive stillness of Henry, longing for the life of a 'homely swain', who might

> sit upon a hill as I do now
> To carve out dials quaintly, point by point,
> Thereby to see the minutes how they run, (2.5.23–5)

despite its virtue in religious terms, signals everything that is wrong with him as a king. Indeed he sits on this molehill not just as an expression of personal choice, but because Margaret and Clifford have 'chid' him away from the battle, 'swearing both | They prosper best of all when I am thence' (17–18). York's aggression and willingness to break his vow are set against Henry's extreme passivity and monastic attitude, and both are found wanting. Images of elevation carry nuances of pride as well as leadership and can also signify ironically, to suggest failure and humiliation. The competing claimants to the English throne are set up in parallel positions spatially, partly to point up the contrast between them, but also to reflect on the extent to which both fall short of ideal kingship. The repeated up-and-down movement, furthermore, the growing sense that elevation to a high place precedes a necessary fall, also mimics the changing fortunes of civil war. One side wins a victory only to cede to the other on the next occasion. The country is torn apart as those who wish to rule it jockey for position. The vertical parallels point up a similar

irony to the strongly horizontal scene discussed in Chapter 3 above
where a father and son find they have slain their own son and father.

Richard II scripts a staging equally strongly focused on the vertical
plane, and bound too into the language of the play. Indeed one often-
quoted image in particular epitomizes the way the whole play is
conceived in terms of rise and fall:

> Now is this golden crown like a deep well
> That owes two buckets, filling one another,
> The emptier ever dancing in the air,
> The other down, unseen, and full of water.
> That bucket down and full of tears am I,
> Drinking my griefs, whilst you mount up on high. (4.1.174–9)

The speaker is Richard; his rival for the throne Bolingbroke; and the
image is first briefly pictured horizontally before the vertical takes
precedence: 'On this side my hand, on that side thine' (173). This
scene, 4.1, is the scene of formal abdication; but the earlier scene at
Flint Castle, where Richard surrenders to Bolingbroke (3.3), is the
key scene in terms of conveying the moment when Bolingbroke gains
ascendancy. As it opens, Bolingbroke and his supporters are at a short
distance from Flint Castle, where Richard is. Northumberland, reporting on Richard's position, calls him simply 'Richard', without the
title 'King', and is immediately rebuked by York. The moment anticipates the real loss of title that is to follow. And that ironic
anticipation is echoed by Bolingbroke's own expressed belief that
the castle 'contains no king' (23). This simple error reverberates
with ominous prescience.

On hearing the news that King Richard is indeed within, Bolingbroke sends a duly respectful message, imaging his duty to his
monarch in terms of lowering his person before him:

> Henry Bolingbroke
> Upon his knees doth kiss King Richard's hand,
> And sends allegiance and true faith of heart
> To his most royal person. (3.3.34–7)

At this point Bolingbroke and his supporters still recognize Richard
as their natural and rightful King. Bolingbroke demands only the
restoration of his lands and the repeal of his banishment. He is still

ready to pay due respect to Richard as King, to 'lay [his] arms and power' at his feet (38). That willingness, however, is not absolute but conditional. Bolingbroke will submit if and only if his banishment is repealed and his lands are restored (39–40).

How then do things move so swiftly towards the abdication of the King? The scripted use of space does much of the work, and it is worth attending to it closely. Bolingbroke's command 'March on, and mark King Richard, how he looks' (60) is immediately followed by a stage direction that indicates his arrival directly beneath the castle walls, and from this point on the tiring-house wall begins to represent the castle wall: '*The trumpets sound [a parley without, and an answer within; then a flourish within.]. King Richard appeareth on the walls, with the Bishop of Carlisle, the Duke of Aumerle [Scrope, and the Earl of Salisbury]*' (60). Richard and his men, then, are situated in the gallery of the tiring-house wall, looking down on Northumberland and his soldiers; and as Northumberland and York look up at Richard the imagery of their response draws on the imagery of sun and eagle, triumphant and elevated images, of a piece with York's remark: 'Yet looks he like a king' (67). (The hint for Richard's physical elevation in this scene perhaps came from Holinshed's brief statement that Richard 'was walking aloft on the brays of the walls' looking out for Bolingbroke, but its metaphorical development towards Richard's descent is Shakespeare's.[6]) At this point, however, the respect due to Richard suddenly starts to be withdrawn, and the withdrawal is all the more evident because the staging, with Richard above and the rebels below, emphasizes the superiority of the King over his subjects and the general expectation that the subjects will also voluntarily enact their obedience by lowering their bodies before their King. What is evident from Richard's first words is that Northumberland refuses to kneel, even though Richard waits for him to do so:

> We are amazed; and thus long have we stood
> To watch the fearful bending of thy knee,
> Because we thought ourself thy lawful king.
> And if we be, how dare thy joints forget
> To pay their aweful duty to our presence? (71–5)

From there, with that revealing past tense ('thought ourself thy lawful king'), Richard moves immediately to a conditional that already begins to compass the possibility of not being his subject's lawful king: 'If we be not, show us the hand of God | That hath dismissed us from our stewardship' (76–7).

The speech is lengthy, and by the end of it Richard has summoned a vision of civil war that will spread the pastures of England with the blood of ten thousand men. Northumberland expresses horror at the suggestion, but offers no apology for failing to kneel. He reiterates Bolingbroke's explicitly humble greeting and his affirmation that he comes for 'no further scope | Than for his lineal royalties' (111–12). Again, like Bolingbroke's statement that the castle contains 'no king', the term 'royalties' reverberates more widely than its immediate meaning. It here means 'hereditary rights'; but it occurs as part of a single long sentence in which, six lines earlier, Northumberland says that Bolingbroke swears by the tomb of their 'royal grandsire' (Edward III) and 'by the royalties of both your bloods' that he has come only for these 'royalties' (rights) now resounding with the same name. The connection between one kind of royalty and the other, even within a context avowing that Bolingbroke does not seek to be King, carries the clear suggestion that one kind of right is linked to the other; and if one is demanded, the other may not be far behind.

To Northumberland, Richard graciously grants Bolingbroke's request, but to Aumerle he immediately voices his reservations about having done so and asks:

> Shall we call back Northumberland, and send
> Defiance to the traitor, and so die? (128–9)

As is clear here, he has granted Bolingbroke's wishes because he fears that to do otherwise would result in his death. As he watches Northumberland return with Bolingbroke's reply, he sees accession to Bolingbroke's demands as the beginning of a downward slope that, while it may save him from death, leads towards deposition:

> What must the King do now? Must he submit?
> The King shall do it. Must he be deposed?
> The King shall be contented. (142–4)

In the long speech that follows, Richard, longing for a hermitage, swiftly becomes reminiscent of Henry VI, who longed to exchange his kingship for the contemplative quiet of a shepherd's life:

> I'll give my jewels for a set of beads,
> My gorgeous palace for a hermitage,
> My gay apparel for an almsman's gown ... (146–8)

The speech is much longer than quoted here, and length is part of its point. Richard's tendency to dwell on himself and his own situation in extensive lyrical speeches is deliberately set against Bolingbroke's briefer and more practical manner of dealing.

By contrast, the visual image of his surrender is sudden, irreversible, and potently emblematic of the shift that this scene has enacted:

> NORTHUMBERLAND My lord, in the base court he doth attend
>   To speak with you. May it please you to come down?
> RICHARD Down, down I come, like glist'ring Phaeton,
>   Wanting the manage of unruly jades.
>   In the base court: base court where kings grow base
>   To come at traitors' calls, and do them grace.
>   In the base court, come down; down court, down King,
>   For night-owls shriek where mounting larks should sing. (175–82)

Bolingbroke's subsequent kneeling to Richard cannot neutralize the overwhelming effect of Richard's descent, and Richard himself is quick to point out the irony and bad faith of the gestus:

>   you debase your princely knee
>   To make the base earth proud with kissing it.
>   ...
>   Up, cousin, up. Your heart is up, I know,
>   This high at least, although your knee be low. (188–93)

The descent from the walls to the base court at Flint Castle is the turning point of the play and a microcosmic visual enactment of its central concern. As a reversal of the tableau placing the monarch at the apex of the social order, familiar from the street pageantry of royal entries, it has all the more power to shock.[7]

Division of the stage picture between vertical planes is especially characteristic of the history play, mainly because of the prevalence of siege scenes. These, like the Flint Castle scene, use the tiring-house wall as the imaginary wall of a city or castle, and those people within the walls usually appear above to those outside besieging them. Like many horizontally divided scenes, vertically divided scenes usually also script opposition, creating an 'us and them' alignment of the audience. *1 Henry VI* is dominated by scenes constructed in this way. It has at least seven scenes situating one group *'above'* (as contemporary stage directions often put it) and the other group below, on the main stage. One effect of this kind of scene is to inspire feelings of national pride and patriotism, perhaps particularly so in time of war, as these plays were first staged when the English were at war. Thomas Nashe, writing in 1592 (of an early play before Shakespeare's on the subject of Henry V), recorded feeling 'what a glorious thing it is to have Henry the Fifth represented on the stage, leading the French king prisoner, and forcing both him and the Dauphin to swear fealty'.[8] But a further effect of repeating that vertically parallel stage picture with such frequency is to show the English and the French tied together in seemingly interminable opposition, and at the same time to show them as almost interchangeable, thereby suggesting that every victory will have its reversal.[9] Even more ironically, civil strife between the English is also staged before the imagined walls of the Tower, implying that internal divisions are as futile and ingrained a pattern of behaviour as hostilities abroad.[10]

On occasion a particular scene can create real complexities for the audience in terms of alignment. *King John* has an extended second scene (occupying the whole of Act 2) which brings together vertical and horizontal opposition in dynamic ways, creating swiftly changing viewing positions for audiences. It opens before the walls of Angers, as King Philip of France's opening remark immediately informs the audience:

> Before Angers well met, brave Austria. (2.1.1)

These are two groups of allies meeting, under the King of France and the Duke of Austria, to enforce the claim to sovereignty over England of Arthur, son of Geoffrey, the elder brother of King John, the present King of England. Their amity, as opposed to enmity, is conveyed through gestures and stage picture as well as language. The two groups come together: Arthur gives his hand to the Duke of Austria, and the Duke kisses Arthur's cheek in return by way of pledging his dedication to the cause. Angers is part of England's territory in France, and the French and Austrian armies are preparing to besiege it. The long opening scene of the play has shown John deciding to go to war to oppose this claim, but at this point the French have not yet had England's answer. Constance, Arthur's mother, is advising them to wait for that answer before laying siege to the city, but at that very moment the French herald arrives with news of England's defiance. No sooner has he announced his message than a drum beats, signalling that the English are at hand. As King John and his followers enter, the two armies who have just entered, presumably from opposite sides of the stage, must now group themselves on one side as the English group themselves on the other.

King John's opening words reinforce the antithesis of the stage picture:

> Peace be to France, if France in peace permit
> Our just and lineal entrance to our town;
> If not, bleed France, and peace ascend to heaven,
> Whiles we, God's wrathful agent, do correct
> Their proud contempt that beats his peace to heaven. (2.1.84–8)

As the tone of the words indicates, there is no coming together of these two groups, but defiant and hostile distance between them, as each affirms the legitimacy of its claim to England. The exchange quickly escalates into insults, and shifts first to the two women, Constance, the mother of Arthur, and Queen Eleanor, the mother of King John. From there it shifts again to a quarrel between the Bastard (introduced in Act 1 as the illegitimate son of King Richard the Lionheart, elder brother to both John and Geoffrey) and the Duke of Austria. Louis, the Dauphin, cuts across both quarrels with the peremptory command: 'Women and fools, break off your conference' (150). The unseemly wrangling between Eleanor and Constance continues, however, until King Philip orders a trumpeter to summon the citizens of Angers to the walls to 'speak | Whose title they admit, Arthur's or John's' (201).

At this point a citizen, possibly the same citizen who is identified as Hubert later in the scene, appears upon the walls.[11] So now the stage picture is divided significantly both horizontally and vertically, with the English and French either side of the stage, and the Citizen centrally and above. The physical positions enact the political situation: England and France are at odds, on the verge of war, and the citizens of Angers hold the balance of power. They must pronounce themselves subjects of one or other monarch. First John, then Philip, speaks at length, each both justifying his claim and threatening Angers with vicious revenge if it supports the opposite monarch. For Angers, the matter is simultaneously simple and complex:

> In brief, we are the King of England's subjects.
> For him, and in his right, we hold this town. (267–8)

But who is the rightful King of England: Arthur or John? The roughly symmetrical patterning of both stage picture and speeches begins to break down at this point as the Bastard punctuates the speech turns of the Citizen and the two kings with a sequence of asides culminating in an open challenge to the Duke of Austria.

The Bastard's role has been to embody challenge and to disrupt symmetry from the start of the play. When he enters, in Act 1, scene 1, he is at odds with his brother and his descent, as the unacknowledged bastard of Richard I. The dispute that he and his brother have brought to court is about their respective rights to inherit from a father who may not have fathered both of them; and Queen Eleanor, seeing in the Bastard a likeness to Richard, her eldest son, offers him a choice:

> Whether hadst thou rather—be a Faulconbridge
> And like thy brother to enjoy thy land,
> Or the reputed son of Coeur-de-Lion,
> Lord of thy presence, and no land beside? (1.1.134–7)

The Bastard chooses to renounce his land and follow the Queen to France, a choice which explains his presence here before the walls of Angers. The challenge of his presence, his adoption of marginality as an active preference rather than a position of inferiority, are confirmed by the way this first scene ends, with the Bastard first in soliloquy, mocking courtly manners and false pretensions, and then in dialogue with his mother, who confirms that he is the son of Richard Coeur-de-Lion. His strength, however, comes from his indomitable sense of self, regardless of descent: 'I am I, howe'er I was begot' (175); and it is no surprise to find him openly cynical about his social superiors and taking pleasure in opposing their easy sense of right and order, thrusting himself in as the natural opponent to the

Duke of Austria, despite the stain on his birth that should debar him from such entitlement.

The stage clears, briefly, as the English and French forces exit 'severally' (that is, through different doors), to battle. 'Excursions' signal offstage fighting, after which the heralds of France and England enter sequentially (and presumably again from opposite doors), each claiming victory.[12] Hubert, centrally positioned on the walls, pronounces them equal in language that parallels the symmetry of their physical placing on the stage:

> Blood hath bought blood, and blows have answered blows;
> Strength matched with strength, and power confronted power.
> Both are alike, and both alike we like. (329–31)

Now the English and French forces enter from opposite sides of the stage (this time specified by the stage direction), ready to renew the battle. The Bastard, ever outside the binary polarities of the two kings, suggests joining forces to assault Angers instead of each other, in a speech that emphasizes the physical make-up of the stage, with its gallery, by explicitly comparing it to a theatre:

> By heaven, these scroyles of Angers flout you, Kings,
> And stand securely on their battlements
> As in a theatre, whence they gape and point
> At your industrious scenes and acts of death. (373–6)

The speech again physically points up the Bastard's own marginality. It is spoken as an observer, of a stage picture which he is almost certainly describing from a peripheral, off-centre position on the stage. His own 'off-centredness' is coded through his representation here of a symmetrical stage picture—a stalemate indeed—from an asymmetrical position of his own, since he stands outside and free of the two groupings of English and French.

His suggestion, however (which he gleefully sees as likely to result in the French shooting each other under their two leaders, Philip and the Duke of Austria, who offer to position themselves north and south of the city), is quickly headed off by the more positive proposal of Hubert, citizen of Angers. His proposal is that the Lady Blanche of England should be married to Louis the Dauphin of France.[13]

Again, verbal patterning highlights symmetry, but now also incorporates the impetus towards bringing opposing halves together:

> He is the half part of a blessèd man,
> Left to be finishèd by such as she,
> And she a fair divided excellence,
> Whose fullness of perfection lies in him. (438–41)

The Bastard's response is cynical in the extreme, and as Hubert's language becomes more highly rhetorical, his becomes more insistently colloquial and critical, highlighting his exclusion from the harmonious picture now in process of being created:

> Zounds, I was never so bethumped with words
> Since I first called my brother's father Dad. (467–8)

The other parties, however, ignore him (and he may indeed speak only to the audience, in an aside implicitly unheard by the other players on stage), and continue to negotiate the match. Louis and Blanche draw physically closer, as they must if union is to resolve enmity, first to look into each other's eyes and whisper together (497–504) and eventually to join hands and kiss, as the match is confirmed (536). Where the focus of the stage picture has hitherto been divided, between right and left and up and down, it now comes together on both planes. As the two sides approach one another with this kiss, King Philip also orders the citizens of Angers to open their gates, allowing the English and French to leave the stage in a single procession rather than 'severally', as they have done throughout the rest of this scene. If this is a stage with three doors, then the central door must have been the exit point of choice here.[14]

All but the Bastard leave the stage. His mocking commentary on the rapprochement going on around him has continued aside, but now Shakespeare chooses to end the scene by focusing on the view from the margin rather than the harmonious exit picture, since this is not a peace that will last. As the Bastard knows, this union is an act of 'commodity' (574ff.) or advantage, 'a most base and vile-concluded peace' (587) agreed for reasons of practical gain, not true reconcilement. For the Bastard, the actions of kings constitute a justification for his own pursuit of individual advantage; and it is on this note that he closes off the scene with a rhyming couplet:

> Since kings break faith upon commodity,
> Gain, be my lord, for I will worship thee![15] (598–9)

Siege scenes, with their emphasis on the vertical divisions of the stage and the political divisions they signify, become less common in Shakespeare's history plays written after 1595. *Henry V*, the last play to be written of the Second Tetralogy, and the last of Shakespeare's history plays before the isolated and much later *Henry VIII*, contains one major scene set before the city walls of Harfleur, but its impact is much more problematic in context than the scenes we have been examining here. It is brief, a mere fifty-eight lines long, and forty-three of those are King Henry's address to the citizens of Harfleur. There is no fighting, no time for any binary feeling of opposition to emerge; but instead, the sense of a single dominant force (Henry) overcoming the obstacle in its way (Harfleur's potential opposition to his entry). The rhetoric is extraordinarily brutal, and the violence threatened is no honourable battle between opposing forces, but slaughter without restraint. Henry threatens that his 'blind and bloody soldier[s]', once loosed from his control (as he fully intends to loose them), will defile the daughters of Harfleur, dash their fathers' heads against the walls, and raise their naked infants 'spitted upon pikes' (3.3.114–18). The only way to avoid this is to yield now; and the Governor does. So the potential symmetry of 'us-and-them' is immediately overwhelmed by a conquest so easy that there is only 'us'; but that 'us' is surely tarnished with a disreputable cast that highlights the one-sidedness of the scene in paradoxical ways. The victory is easy, but the victors look less than glorious. It is perhaps not accidental that Shakespeare chooses the open field of Agincourt for Henry's more heroic speech before battle (4.3.18–67). Scenes before city-gates have, over the course of Shakespeare's prior history plays, become too often ironized to be used by this time as a forum for heroism.

Symbolic Objects and the Ceremonial Body

Ceremony, as is evident from preceding chapters, is a central feature of courts and kingship. It is also, like a play, a mode of performance, structured and ritualistic, paying careful attention to costume, props, setting, and tempo. In a history play, furthermore, as well as in life, it forms a crucial element in the way history is constructed and remembered, since it furnishes striking and memorable visual images and sensory experiences. History becomes a sequence of key moments, many of which bear a strong resemblance to one another, so that each coronation, deathbed, or funeral, for example, both resembles those that have gone before it, is distinguished from them in important ways, and is replayed and reworked in subsequent variations on those themes. This is as true of Hall or Holinshed as it is of Shakespeare. The same ceremonies recur in the chronicles as in the dramatizations of their narratives. History, especially as the Tudor chroniclers told it, with a strong emphasis on the monarchy and the court, was eminently translatable to the stage. Shakespeare's stage directions, as well as his dialogue, are sometimes lifted word for word from the chronicle sources.

Thus, the ceremonial objects of history—crown, throne, sceptre, robes, and so on—become the symbolic objects that draw the spectator's gaze on stage, and the narrative of history is typically structured around the movement and positioning of these objects. Passing the crown from hand to hand on stage becomes an ongoing emblem for civil war and the struggle for power, just as the physical ascent or descent of the throne marks the shift from one rule to another. As Michael Hattaway notes, 'In Elizabethan English, the word "ceremony" could mean both a ceremonial occasion and a talismanic object used therein.'[1] And such 'ceremonies' are not only heavily invested with political and even religious significance in themselves; they also put certain constraints on actors' postures, gestures, and movements. Wearing a crown or a heavy trailing robe, for example, dictates an erect and dignified stance or movement, just as sitting in a throne dictates a conscious, upright, and expansive way of sitting; and the effect of mocking these objects with substitutes like a paper crown or a molehill (Chapters 3 and 4 above) is made visible to the audience partly through the difference an actor's body registers in responding to the (literally) light weight, triviality, and absurdity of these substitutes.

Performing history through its ceremonial aspect, through the specialized set of props and costumes that belong to ceremony, scripts a reverence towards particular types of person and event. Equally, then, disrupting or casualizing ceremony also performs certain attitudes towards history. Too much or too casual handling of symbolic objects can evacuate their symbolic charge; and implicitly casting aspersions on ceremony makes way for the possibility of scepticism or irreverence in the audience. This is the case, for example, when, against the advice of his nobles, King John has himself recrowned between Act 4, scene 1 and Act 4, scene 2 in the play of that name. As he ascends the throne, his 'once again' already seems to tarnish the sacramental nature of coronation, and Pembroke's reply confirms its jarring and mistaken tone:

> KING JOHN   Here once again we sit, once again crowned,
>   And looked upon, I hope, with cheerful eyes.
> PEMBROKE   This 'once again', but that your highness pleased,
>   Was once superfluous. You were crowned before,
>   And that high royalty was ne'er plucked off. (*King John*, 4.2.1–5)

Later in this scene the Bastard reports Peter of Pomfret's prophecy:

> That ere the next Ascension Day at noon,
> Your highness should deliver up your crown. (151–2)

But even this doom-laden prophecy is trivialized in the event. The crown is passed from hand to hand between King and Cardinal like an everyday object, as John, previously excommunicated, returns to the fold of the Church:

> KING JOHN   Thus have I yielded up into your hand
>   The circle of my glory.
> CARDINAL PANDULPH   (*handing the crown to John*) Take again
>   From this my hand, as holding of the Pope,
>   Your sovereign greatness and authority. (5.1.1–4)

Despite the elevated rhetoric that seeks to position the crown as a 'circle of . . . glory' and an emblem of 'sovereign greatness and authority', the effect of handing over the crown only to have it immediately handed back again is one of bathos. The crown, and John's authority, look ridiculous. Such brief and reduced ceremony as there may be in this moment functions as a cynical reflection on the operations of power and the petty quarrels of kings and popes.

Elsewhere, however, symbolic props may accrete a more intense charge as the play develops, and this is the case with Duke Humphrey's staff of office in *2 Henry VI*. Almost certainly Humphrey, Duke of Gloucester, Lord Protector of England, must carry his staff of office in the opening scene of the play, which is a ceremonial court scene opening with a flourish of trumpets and a processional entry from two sides of the stage. A formal opening was a useful device for a history play, since costumes, insignia, rank order of entry, and props like the Protector's staff made it easier for the audience to identify who was who. Such props, identifying role and authority, had inherent symbolic value, both in terms of individual identity and in terms of the state in which they bore office. Humphrey's dream, recounted in the next scene, constructs the staff of office as emblematic both of good rule in the state of England and of Humphrey's own personal devotion to the state:

> Methought this staff, mine office-badge in court,
> Was broke in twain—by whom I have forgot,
> But, as I think, it was by th'Cardinal—
> And on the pieces of the broken wand
> Were placed the heads of Edmund, Duke of Somerset,
> And William de la Pole, first Duke of Suffolk. (1.2.25–30)

To the Duchess of Gloucester, Humphrey's wife, this is 'nothing but an argument | That he that breaks a stick of Gloucester's grove | Shall lose his head for his presumption' (33–5); but audiences at this time would have known that dreams did not figure in plays unless their symbolic or prophetic import was significant (see further Chapter 8 below).

The dream becomes material in Act 2, scene 3, another ceremonial scene in which the King and court come together to pass sentence on the Duchess, condemned to three days' open penance and perpetual banishment for treason. As his wife is taken off by guards, Duke Humphrey expresses his grief and shame and asks the King's permission to leave the court temporarily. The King's response takes Humphrey by surprise:

> Stay, Humphrey Duke of Gloucester. Ere thou go,
> Give up thy staff. Henry will to himself
> Protector be; and God shall be my hope,
> My stay, my guide, and lantern to my feet. (2.3.22–5)

The staff itself becomes the focus of the power struggle whereby Queen Margaret, who is behind the young King's decision to rule the kingdom himself, without a Protector, expresses her hostility to the Duke of Gloucester. Gloucester has from the start of the play seen Margaret as representing everything England has lost by the terms of the marriage treaty with France that brought her to England as Henry's wife. Peremptorily, she orders him here: 'Give up your staff, sir, and the King his realm' (31); and Humphrey, obedient to his King, lays the staff at his feet:

> My staff? Here, noble Henry, is my staff.
> As willingly do I the same resign
> As ere thy father Henry made it mine;
> And even as willingly at thy feet I leave it
> As others would ambitiously receive it. (32–6)

In comments that follow, the staff, still lying on the ground, comes to seem a part of Humphrey's own body, 'a limb lopped off' (42); but someone, possibly Margaret, or even Henry himself, must pick it up off the ground and put it into Henry's hand, since Margaret then observes:

> This staff of honour raught, there let it stand,
> Where it best fits to be, in Henry's hand. (43–4)

Thus, when Suffolk says: 'Thus droops this lofty pine and hangs his sprays' (45), the distinction between the Protector and his staff is so far elided that it is impossible to say whether the image of the drooping pine refers primarily to Humphrey or his staff.

Attention then shifts immediately, within the same scene, to the trial by combat appointed between an armourer, one Horner, accused by his servant of treasonous speech, and the servant, Peter, who accuses him. Their weapons are staffs with sandbags tied to them, grotesque parodies of the staff given such serious prominence immediately before, and the context is both comic and serious. The stage direction scripts their entry in extraordinary detail, as a class-based parody of a chivalric trial by combat (such as the one prepared for at the opening of *Richard II*):[2]

Enter at one door Horner the armourer and his Neighbours, drinking to him so much that he is drunk; and he enters with a drummer before him and [carrying] his staff with a sandbag fastened to it. Enter at the other door Peter his man, also with a drummer and a staff with sandbag, and Prentices drinking to him. (58)

Such an entry is scripted to strip all dignity from the proceedings, despite the fact that this will be a fight to the death, and the cacophony of neighbours urging both participants to drink more reinforces that sense of the event bursting out of its formal constraints to produce comic chaos. The Earl of Salisbury has to cut across the noise to get the combat under way: 'Come, leave your drinking, and fall to blows' (80). His attempt to bring the proceedings to order, however, at once relapses into comedy as he asks Peter his name and is told: 'Thump' (84). Even the Earl then cannot resist a jokey reply: 'Thump! Then see thou thump thy master well' (85).

The fight finally goes ahead, and Henry presumably remains holding the staff of honour that represents Humphrey's honest service to the state while Horner and Peter flail around with their own staffs, weighted with sandbags, lumpen mockeries of the lances of knightly combat as well as of Humphrey's noble staff of office. Yet regardless of their foolish aspect, these crude weapons can and do kill. Peter strikes Horner down and he confesses to treason as he dies.

Peter's register is immediately elevated to a different rhetorical level as he realizes he has 'proved' his master's guilt:

> O God, have I overcome mine enemy in this presence?
> O Peter, thou hast prevailed in right; (98–9)

and Henry endorses his pronouncement by making a formal statement of judgment:

> Go, take hence that traitor from our sight,
> For by his death we do perceive his guilt.
> And God in justice hath revealed to us
> The truth and innocence of this poor fellow,
> Which he had thought to have murdered wrongfully. (100–4)

Whether an audience really feels, or is intended to feel, that divine justice has been revealed through this drunken and brutish encounter is a moot point. The high rhetoric is at odds with the stage picture of two men hitting each other with sandbags on staffs.

Perhaps the most daring and edgy scene of this kind is the tavern scene in *1 Henry IV*. Here it is the most familiar—but also the most sacred—objects of ceremony that are parodied: the chair of state and the crown, with the addition of the sceptre. Prince Henry (Hal), anticipating his father's wrath when he is called before him the next day, decides to play out the interview in jest with Falstaff in the tavern:

PRINCE HENRY Do thou stand for my father and examine me upon the particulars of my life.
FALSTAFF Shall I? Content. This chair shall be my state, this dagger my sceptre, and this cushion my crown.
He sits. (2.4.363–6)

The Prince, however, immediately questions the conventions of theatre, by which cheap props are accepted by audiences as the objects they represent, and evacuates the representation by reducing it to its literal components:

Thy state is taken for a joint-stool, thy golden sceptre for a leaden dagger, and thy precious rich crown for a pitiful bald crown. (367–9)

Yet Falstaff, despite taking up and extending the explicit references to the fact that this is theatre, vows to move him:

Well, an [if] the fire of grace be not quite out of thee, now thou shalt be moved. Give me a cup of sack to make my eyes look red, that it may be thought I have wept; for I must speak in passion, and I will do it in King Cambyses' vein. (370–4)

It is a vow seemingly made in jest, with a knowing contempt for an older theatrical tradition of high passion and ranting rhetoric (as in the tragedy of *King Cambyses* (*c.*1558–69)); yet audiences may find themselves indeed moved in a different way by this scene as it reaches its very serious climax 100 lines further on.

In the meantime Falstaff plays the part of Hal's father, at first with parodic excess, in quasi-tragic mode, reducing the Hostess to tears of laughter:

FALSTAFF Weep not, sweet queen, for trickling tears are vain.
HOSTESS O, the Father, how he holds his countenance!
FALSTAFF For God's sake, lords, convey my tristful queen,
    For tears do stop the floodgates of her eyes.
HOSTESS O Jesu, he doth it as like one of these harlotry players as ever I see!
(378–83)

Falstaff begins to grow into the part, away from straightforward parody into more daring satire, as he begins to skirt the subject of the Prince's companions, before making the ultimate comic move: advising the Prince to banish all his companions except the virtuous and goodly Falstaff: 'Him keep with, the rest banish' (414–15). But it is at this point that Hal loses patience with the way the game is going, and reverses the roles, despite Falstaff's protest that the Prince will not play the part of the King 'half so gravely, so majestically' (419–20). In this second version of the King's address to his son the Prince's tone is indeed neither grave nor majestic, but abusive, and potentially increasingly venomous, depending on the delivery:

There is a devil haunts thee in the likeness of an old fat man; a tun of man is thy companion. Why dost thou converse with that trunk of humours, that bolting-hutch of beastliness, that swollen parcel of dropsies, that huge bombard of sack, that stuffed cloak-bag of guts, that roasted Manningtree ox with the pudding in his belly, that reverend Vice, that grey iniquity, that father ruffian, that vanity in years? (431–8)

Falstaff, taking his cue from the Prince, raises the rhetorical stakes with an extended set of repetitions, semi-comic in themselves, but climaxing in a plea that can scarcely avoid sounding the ring of truth, however jovial the delivery:

No, my good lord, banish Peto, banish Bardolph, banish Poins; but for sweet Jack Falstaff, kind Jack Falstaff, true Jack Falstaff, valiant Jack Falstaff, and therefore more valiant being as he is old Jack Falstaff, banish not him thy Harry's company, banish not him thy Harry's company—banish plump Jack and banish all the world. (456–62)

The Prince changes the tone in a moment by puncturing rhetorical excess with terrible simplicity: 'I do, I will' (463). The knocking at the door as the Sheriff and his men arrive cuts off any further development, but the threat is out in the open, left hanging. Just as Falstaff vowed at the start of the miniature play to move the Prince if he has not quite lost 'the fire of grace', so the Prince vows here to banish Falstaff. He, then, is seemingly unmoved by Falstaff's plea, but the scripting of this vicious little game invites audiences to be moved in contrary ways: to laughter, to sympathy, to condemnation, and, finally, to uncertain anticipation. From this point on, they will be waiting for the banishment of Falstaff.

It will not come, however, until the next play; and this is one of the strongest pieces of evidence that Shakespeare was writing this play, at least, in the expectation of also writing its sequel. Not only does Falstaff's banishment finally come in the closing scene of *2 Henry IV* (see Chapter 2 above); the play also takes up the heavy symbolic significance of the crown, prepared for by the cushion in this scene, in order to complicate the relationship between the Prince and his father given in cartoon shape in this scene, where the true focus is on the relationship between Hal and his substitute-father, Falstaff. In *2 Henry IV* the scene is set in the King's bedchamber, where the King lies sick and dying in his bed. As he removes the crown and instructs it to be set upon the pillow ('Set me the crown upon my pillow here' (*2 Henry IV*, 4.3.137)), that very placing may call up faint echoes of the cushion that served as crown in the earlier play. Crowns, of course, when not on the heads of kings, were usually carried on ceremonial cushions, so the use of a cushion to stand for a crown in *1 Henry IV* was already a synecdoche rather than a random choice of prop.

Here in *2 Henry IV* the pillow of a sick bed is also already reminiscent of the ceremonial cushion as well as marking its ironic difference from that object. If audiences do not pick up echoes of the comic cushion on Falstaff's head when the crown is first placed on the pillow they may well do so a few lines later, when all withdraw from the stage except the sick King and the Prince, whose attention is immediately drawn to it:

> Why doth the crown lie there upon his pillow,
> Being so troublesome a bedfellow? (152–3)

For the Prince, as the crown lies beside his father's head on the pillow, the crown becomes the focus of a meditation on kingship that distracts from the painful and personal focus of his relationship with his father while at the same time running in tandem with it. Like Humphrey's staff, the prop is not the man, but neither is it wholly separate from him. More importantly, furthermore, it is here a prop that brings together a king and his son, since it represents the kingship that one will inherit from the other. The Prince, indeed, casts his filial duty in a relationship of exchange with his inheritance of the crown:

> Thy due from me
> Is tears and heavy sorrows of the blood,
> Which nature, love, and filial tenderness
> Shall, O dear father, pay thee plenteously.
> My due from thee is this imperial crown,
> Which, as immediate from thy place and blood,
> Derives itself to me. (168–74)

As he imagines this exchange of obligations, he further imagines the crown passing from head to head, and translates this into a literal gesture, putting the crown on his own head; and as he leaves the bedchamber with the crown on his head he promises not only to protect 'this lineal honour' against even 'the world's whole strength', but to leave it to his descendants, 'as 'tis left to me' (175–8). For the King, however, waking to find the empty space on the pillow, the Prince's imaginative leap is inaccessible and he calls for Warwick, Gloucester, and Clarence in high anxiety, wanting to know who removed the crown from his pillow. For the audience too, especially an early modern audience, the Prince's act of taking the crown from its rightful wearer and putting it on his own head is close to sacrilegious. Monarchs do not try on crowns like so many hats. The crown is a sacred object, identifying the peculiar status of a king or queen; and the moment when the crown passes from one monarch to the next is literally a consecrated one, embedded in the ceremony of coronation, at the heart of which the new monarch makes solemn vows and is anointed with holy oil before the crown is set upon his head. He does not simply pick it up and put it on, and it is not his place or right to do so. The crown sits on the altar through most of the service and is ceremonially placed on the new monarch's head by the Archbishop of Canterbury after the new King has sworn his duty to God and the kingdom. To try it on and walk off with it is an affront to the custom-hallowed sanctity of the object (though Shakespeare's history plays, as we have seen, several times script the inappropriate handling of the crown to emphasize the unseemliness of particular power struggles).

In the same way as the mishandling of ceremonial or sacramental objects seems to threaten to downgrade their symbolic value, so more everyday objects can be handled and presented in such a way as to increase their symbolic value. Thus, for example, the gloves that Henry V and the soldier Michael Williams exchange the night before Agincourt in token of their quarrel seem at that point, to Williams at least, to be mere markers of their identity for future mutual recognition. Williams, of course, does not know that his quarrel (which is about the King, and whether his word can be trusted, having sworn he will not be ransomed) is also *with* the King, who is in disguise. Each takes the other's glove to wear in his cap (4.1). After the great victory of Agincourt, Henry sees Williams wearing the glove in his cap and summons him to explain it. On hearing that Williams has sworn an oath to fight with the possessor of his glove, Henry and Fluellen, who is with him, agree that he should keep his oath. Henry then constructs another layer of deceit to add to his earlier disguise by giving Fluellen the glove that Williams gave him and telling him he plucked it from the French Duke of Alençon's helmet in battle. He asks Fluellen to 'wear this favour for me' and to apprehend any man that challenges it as a friend to Alençon and an enemy to Henry (4.7).

When Williams and Fluellen next meet, Williams recognizes Fluellen's glove, but Fluellen does not recognize the glove that Williams wears:

WILLIAMS Sir, know you this glove?
FLUELLEN Know the glove? I know the glove is a glove.
WILLIAMS I know this (*plucking the glove from Fluellen's cap*), and thus I challenge it.
He strikes Fluellen. (4.8.6–9)

By this point, to say 'the glove is a glove' is to point up the irony of Williams's error. The glove may look like any other glove (just as the King in disguise looked like any other man), but as the King's glove it has special significance; and it accrues more significance, including distorted and misleading associations, as it travels from hand to hand and from scene to scene. Tempers rise following the blow, but the quarrel is quickly arrested as first the Earl of Warwick and the Duke of Gloucester, then King Henry and the Duke of Exeter, intervene. Williams and Fluellen, each set up in different ways for this fight by the King, give their accounts of having done as they promised to do when they saw the respective gloves; but for Henry this is a moment of pure theatre:

> Give me thy glove, soldier. Look, here is the fellow of it.
> 'Twas I indeed thou promisèd'st to strike,
> And thou hast given me most bitter terms. (39–42)

He continues briefly accusing Williams of offences against him, but as Williams rightly replies:

Your majesty came not like yourself. You appeared to me but as a common man. Witness the night, your garments, your lowliness. And what your highness suffered under that shape, I beseech you take it for your own fault, and not mine, for had you been as I took you for, I made no offence. (49–55)

Again, the occasion gives Henry the opportunity to create a further moment of pure theatre, by which the glove and, supposedly, the offence are both magically transformed:

Here, Uncle Exeter, fill this glove with crowns
And give it to this fellow.—Keep it, fellow,
And wear it for an honour in thy cap
Till I do challenge it. (56–9)

This creates a slightly queasy effect. On the one hand it seems to seek audience approval for a gesture of regal magnanimity (awkwardly akin perhaps, for later audiences, to the kind of flourish whereby the fairy godmother transforms the pumpkin into a coach in *Cinderella*); but on the other hand, Williams's speech of justification is inserted to make an audience see that Henry's talk of 'offence' is out of order. Henry thus 'forgives' an offence that was never truly committed. Characteristically for this play, the effect is dialogic, leaving audiences uncertain whether this is evidence of a man worthy to be king or one who knows how to dazzle with a cheap trick.

Certain objects run right through the history plays accumulating ceremonial implications. Crown and state are the most obvious, but a few others are also significant. Roses, for example, permeate the language and stage pictures of the First Tetralogy, which ends with Henry, Earl of Richmond's, resolution to 'unite the white rose and the red' (*Richard III*, 5.7.19). Sick-chairs (carrying a character on in a chair was a way of demonstrating sickness) are another recurrent element, importantly linked to the recurrence of the throne as a visible prop, and Alan Dessen has shown how the linking of these two in the early history plays conveys powerful messages about disorder, misrule, and 'sickness' in the kingdom.[3] Entry in a sick-chair comes to constitute a kind of anti-ceremony. Equally, because the subject matter of the history plays regularly centres on violence, whether in murder or battle, dead bodies and severed heads are powerful recurrent stage images. Characters enter carrying severed heads either in their hands or raised high on spears; they enter or exit carrying dead bodies; they sit to cradle their loved ones as they die; or even, in one particularly grotesque scene, cradle their severed heads (see Chapter 6 below). Such sequences can interrupt and disrupt ceremonies, or they can constitute a form of ceremony in themselves. The entry or exit with a dead body has its own pace and shape, its own form of funereal spectacle; and walking on stage with a severed head held high similarly constitutes a brief triumphal entry, taking sudden and necessary precedence over whatever else may have been happening on stage.

Finally, it is worth considering the effect of a character who routinely maltreats ceremony: Richard III. As John Jowett writes: 'Nothing is more typical of Richard than his puncturing of ceremony, his disruption and distortion of formal rhetoric, his disrespect for convention, and his attrition of order in all its aspects.'[4] The second scene of the play focuses on the funeral procession of Henry VI, and opens with the hearse borne in, accompanied by Lady Anne, who was betrothed to Henry's son Edward, also now dead. Like the funeral scene that opens *1 Henry VI*, this ceremonial scene is also disrupted, but even more abruptly. Lady Anne, having uttered one speech of mourning, orders the bearers to raise the hearse, and it is at this point that Richard, Duke of Gloucester, enters. His first words are a counter-command: 'Stay, you that bear the corpse, and set it down' (*Richard III*, 1.2.31). Both Anne and the gentlemen bearing the hearse try to insist, but Richard's aggression is too powerful to overcome. So outrageous, however, is this intrusion of the man who slew both Henry VI and his son on the ceremony of Henry's obsequies that the corpse's wounds begin to bleed afresh even in the coffin. The idea that this man should become the lover of Anne seems impossible to contemplate, but Richard turns the ceremony of mourning into one of wooing, making the violation of ceremony into a new and opportunistic ceremony centred on the props of sword and ring. As Anne pours scorn on Richard's claim to love her he finally kneels before her, gives her his sword, and lays his breast open for her to kill him:

> Nay, do not pause, 'twas I that killed your husband;
> But 'twas thy beauty that provokèd me.
> Nay, now dispatch, 'twas I that killed King Henry;
> But 'twas thy heavenly face that set me on.
> *Here she lets fall the sword*
> Take up the sword again or take up me. (1.2.165–9)

This is the turning point, and within a few lines Anne has accepted Richard's ring. As so often, the handling of talismanic objects scripts the key transitions of the play.

The knowingness with which Richard handles objects and stage pictures, however, makes him stand out amongst the characters of the early histories. No stage pictures of which he is a part are accidental. The most outrageous, after the wooing scene, is his show of piety following the death of his brother, Edward IV. By the time the Mayor and Citizens of London arrive to invite him to be England's next king, the audience already knows how he will appear and how calculated the picture is, because Shakespeare scripts Buckingham's direction of it in advance:

> And look you get a prayer book in your hand,
> And stand betwixt two churchmen, good my lord,
> For on that ground I'll build a holy descant.
> Be not easily won to our request.
> Play the maid's part: say 'no', but take it. (3.7.42–6)

Thus, when Richard appears above between two bishops, the outcome is a foregone conclusion. The Mayor points to his position between two clergymen; Buckingham moralizes the prayer book as well as the attendants; Richard pretends unwillingness, and finally accepts the crown, agreeing to be crowned 'Even when you will, since you will have it so' (225).[5] The ceremonial shape that structures the stage picture, and indeed the scene, would be the same whether constructed with sincere or malicious intent, though for the audience the effect is very different. The insight this kind of scene permits into the machiavellian scheming that may underlie the authority of kings, its open representation of the rise to monarchical status as the result of strategy rather than divine entitlement, creates a position for the audience that is as sceptical and knowing as Richard's own. Far from being the adoring subjects that coronations and royal entries seek to manufacture, the spectators of Shakespeare's history plays are free to ask hard questions and to be cynical about the quasi-divinity of kings.

Bodies and Objects in Domestic Space

Having looked in Chapter 5 at how actors and props are constructed by and for ceremonial space, we are now in a position to compare those ways of being with ways of being in domestic space and to reflect on how differently bodies and objects function in domestic scenes. This analysis of 'domestic' scenes, however, is not primarily driven by location. It is true that most of these scenes will be located in implied indoor and household environments, but others will not be identifiably located at all, and are identified as 'domestic' here by the nature of the interaction they portray. Thus, for example, when young Arthur pleads for his life in *King John* (4.1), the location is not specified, and is probably a prison (since we are told in the previous scene that Arthur is John's prisoner, and the entry of executioners bearing a rope and irons further indicates a prison as the likely location). But the scene is domestic because of the highly personal interaction between Arthur and Hubert, whose task it is to have Arthur put to death. Hubert's gentleness of address is the first indication that this is to be no pitiless murder, such as the murder of Macduff's children in *Macbeth*. Hubert's first words to Arthur are 'Young lad, come forth; I have to say with you'; and when Arthur replies politely, and probably warmly: 'Good morrow, Hubert', Hubert's own warmth is evident: 'Good morrow, little prince' (4.1.8–9). The diminutives and the use of personal names script a kindness between them; and the delivery of such kind words necessitates a bodily demeanour that is non-aggressive and approachable.

Arthur's first concern is for Hubert: 'You are sad' (11); and this remark also scripts a degree of physical proximity between Hubert and Arthur and a frankness and directness of gaze on Arthur's part. As the dialogue moves towards open talk of affection and personal relationship ('I would to God | I were your son, so you would love me, Hubert' (23–4)), the function of the scene becomes evident. Hubert, who already finds his task invidious, is increasingly moved to mercy by Arthur's 'innocent prate' (25). The commands of kings, which have a certain weight and necessity in state rooms or other spaces of political authority and negotiation, can seem monstrous and inhuman in more private and personal spaces.

Like the pageant scenes discussed in Chapter 2, domestic scenes are often, strictly speaking, excessive, extraneous to need and additions to the chronicle sources. They exist in order to show a perspective that is unavailable in the kind of scene that moves the plot on, and to allow, even compel, the audience to consider the implications of the decisions and actions taken in more plot-driven scenes. Very often they include women or children as a way of insisting on an alternative perspective to the predominantly male world of politics, battle, and the struggle for power. As Valerie Traub argues, Shakespeare's history plays 'do not merely exclude women; they *stage* the elimination of women from the historical process (an exclusion that *is* the historical process), thus exhibiting the kinds of repressions a phallocentric culture requires to maintain and reproduce itself'.[1] Thus many of these scenes show women seated, quietly involved in mundane activities, talking amongst themselves, singing or listening to music, working with their hands, and generally carrying on the important business of everyday living and maintaining the bonds of family and service. As David Bevington notes, Shakespeare's women 'visually define through their clothes and hand properties a world alternative to that of men', and their roles are remarkably strongly focused on 'the making, wearing, and sewing of clothes or embroidery. The use of needle and thread helps portray their largely passive role (especially in the history plays), their vulnerability to male stratagems, their perseverance, their reliance on one another.'[2] Thus, for example, Queen Katherine sits sewing with her women in *Henry VIII* and asks one of them to sing for her to lighten her troubled soul (3.1).

Not all female roles are like this, however, even in the history plays, and those more assertive or aggressive women who appear in military or power-based scenes, outside the realm of 'women's work', are the more likely to be construed as unnatural or out of place because of the domestic context in which women constructed as admirable in the history plays are usually set. Such assertive women are more in evidence in the early history plays. Joan of Arc, for example, in *1 Henry VI* (or 'Joan Puzel', as the Folio text calls her), is never portrayed in domestic scenes, but only in scenes of power-mongering or battle, and the play very literally demonizes her by showing her as more witch than saint. (The word 'Puzel' or 'Pucelle' in English usage meant both maid or girl and slut or whore. In French its primary meaning was 'virgin'.[3]) She is first called a witch by Talbot when he feels his strength and courage draining from him in battle against her (1.6.6), and her victory at Orléans has the effect of unmanning him ('The shame hereof will make me hide my head', he says (1.6.39)). Set against the most heroic figure of the play in this way, her own manly action and aggressive demeanour invited an early modern audience to condemn her, as did her foreignness and her loose sexual behaviour. Her invocation of devils later in the play (5.3) further situated her as a witch or similar for Shakespeare's audiences (see Chapter 8 below).

Most notable amongst the dominating women of the early history plays is Queen Margaret, described in Hall's Chronicle as 'desirous of glory and covetous of honour, and of reason, policy, counsel, and other gifts and talents of nature belonging to a man'.[4] Characteristically she is represented as raging, cursing, or fighting for her rights on stage. She is never seen sewing, rarely even sitting, but usually in swift, fierce movement, making things happen. She routinely takes decisive, high-handed, often cruel actions: she tears up the commoners' petitions to Humphrey of Gloucester and fulminates against Henry VI's willingness to submit himself to Gloucester's protection (*2 Henry VI*, 1.3.40–65); she boxes the Duchess of Gloucester's ear (*2 Henry VI*, 1.3.139); she divorces herself from her husband's bed when she finds out he has renounced their son's right to inherit the throne (*3 Henry VI*, 1.1.248–51); she taunts Richard of York with a cloth dipped in the blood of his dead son (*3 Henry VI*, 1.4.79–83); she stabs York himself and orders his head to be set on the gates of York (*3 Henry VI*, 1.4.176–80). But there are occasions when even this woman's actions are suddenly domesticated in surprising ways, and her stage presence shifts from the active, swift movements of rage and violence to a still tableau that frames her differently. When Suffolk, depicted as her lover in *2 Henry VI*, dies, the opening stage direction Act 4, scene 4 scripts her to enter the stage carrying his severed head, surrounded by others ignoring her grief: '*Enter King Henry* [*reading*] *a supplication, and Queen Margaret with Suffolk's head, the Duke of Buckingham, and the Lord Saye,* [*with others*]'.[5] The first words spoken are Margaret's:

> Oft have I heard that grief softens the mind,
> And makes it fearful and degenerate;
> Think therefore on revenge and cease to weep.
> But who can cease to weep and look on this?
> Here may his head lie on my throbbing breast,
> But where's the body that I should embrace? (1–6)

and they are immediately followed by Buckingham's address to King Henry:

> What answer makes your grace to the rebels' supplication? (7)

The implication is that Margaret's words are an aside, unheard by others on stage; but the effect is of political life insouciantly continuing, blind to the personal griefs that are its consequence. Both discursively and physically, Margaret is set apart from everything going on around her, where more commonly she is insistently and forcefully part of it. She stands or sits still, either cradling the head like a baby close to her breast or holding it to face her ('Hath this lovely face | Ruled like a wandering planet over me?' (13–14)), while Henry and his lords continue to discuss the rebels.

Finally, at line 20, Henry notices Margaret:

> HENRY   How now, madam?
>   Still lamenting and mourning Suffolk's death?
>   I fear me, love, if that I had been dead,
>   Thou wouldest not have mourned so much for me.
> MARGARET No my love, I should not mourn, but die for thee. (20–4)

The reply is barbed with irony. As the audience is well aware, Margaret would indeed not mourn for her Henry. But the still, yet fierce, tableau of her grief for Suffolk dominates this opening section of the scene and sets both Margaret herself and the political life of the nation in a new light. It also sets the severed head, a recurrent prop in the history plays, in a newly affectionate, even quasi-maternal context, lovingly cradled rather than held up in triumph.

Motherhood is in fact one of the most significant aspects of women's roles in the history plays. Mothers bring forth future kings, they produce daughters who marry kings, and they lose their children to battle, sickness, or murder. They are also in some sense the litmus test of their children's worth, for if a mother condemns or curses her own son, as the Duchess of York condemns her son Richard III (see Chapter 8 below), the son must be wicked indeed. One of the most curious variations on a domestic scene is the scene in *Richard III* where three mothers come together in unlikely unison, all grieving for sons lost to violent deaths. The scene opens with old Queen Margaret alone, returned from exile in France 'To watch the waning of mine adversaries' and hoping to enjoy the revenge of seeing 'bitter, black and tragical' consequences come upon her enemies (4.4.4–7). She draws aside then as Queen Elizabeth (wife of Edward IV and mother of the young princes murdered in the Tower) enters with the Duchess of York (mother of Edward IV, Richard III, and two slaughtered brothers, the Dukes of Rutland and Clarence, and grandmother of the princes in the Tower). As Elizabeth weeps for her lost children, Margaret speaks aside, reminding the audience of her own losses. The God who seemingly slept while Elizabeth's sons were murdered must also have slept, says Margaret, 'When holy Harry [her husband, Henry VI] died, and my sweet son' (20). The Queen and the Duchess sit down together to mourn, wishing that England could 'as well afford a grave | As . . yield a melancholy seat' (25–6), and as their mourning rises in patterned utterances of equal length Margaret too comes forward to add her woes to theirs. If she sits with them, this already represents an unusual posture for her, one that aligns her with these women she has so long been set against. The scene is simultaneously 'domestic', in the sense that it deals with the private life of the emotions and private exchanges between women; ritualistic, in that it begins to sculpt a repetitive, patterned shape out of these three women's sorrows; and typological, in that it recalls the three Marys lamenting in the earlier tradition of the mystery cycles.[6]

Margaret, though she does not cease to be the enemy of the Queen and the Duchess of York, becomes a willing catalyst for their grief, and an active participant in their tableau of mourning, drawing out clear parallels between all three of them despite their enmity:

> MARGARET Tell over your woes again by viewing mine.
> I had an Edward, till a Richard killed him.
> I had a Harry, till a Richard killed him.
> (*To the Queen*) Thou hadst an Edward, till a Richard killed him.
> Thou hadst a Richard, till a Richard killed him.
> DUCHESS OF YORK I had a Richard too, and thou didst kill him.
> I had a Rutland too, thou holp'st to kill him. (36–42)

Motherhood here becomes an especial cross to bear for the Duchess of York, who has not only lost sons and grandsons, but who also produced the very Richard who killed most of them. As Margaret unsparingly reminds her:

> From forth the kennel of thy womb hath crept
> A hell-hound that doth hunt us all to death. (44–5)

The scene rises to a climax as the Queen begs Margaret to teach her how to curse, and Margaret exits with the assurance that Elizabeth's own grief will be the teacher:

> QUEEN My words are dull. O quicken them with thine.
> MARGARET Thy woes will make them sharp and pierce like mine. (118–19)

Grief is not always so cruel or so vengeful in its depiction, however. In a very different kind of scene, now often cut from productions of *2 Henry IV*, Hotspur's widow Kate, Lady Percy, is chastised by her father-in-law, the Earl of Northumberland, for being 'troublesome' (2.3.4). This already scripts a posture for her that is not passive sitting, nor has she been a passive woman in the earlier play, *1 Henry IV*. Both she and Lady Northumberland, Northumberland's wife, are urging Northumberland not to return to war. They are thus trying to intervene in men's affairs, however non-aggressively. They may thus stand or occasionally kneel in this scene, but not sit, since their aim is to change the direction of the action. For women the point at issue in war is death. For men it is honour, as Northumberland makes explicit:

> Alas, sweet wife, my honour is at pawn,
> And, but my going, nothing can redeem it. (7–8)

In the only scene in which she appears in this play, Lady Percy speaks at length in an attempt to persuade the Earl not to return to war, reminding both him and the audience of the damage war has done to her family, and of the unreliability of honour in ensuring any successful outcome:

> The time was, father, that you broke your word
> When you were more endeared to it than now,
> When your own Percy, when my heart's dear Harry
> Threw many a northward look to see his father
> Bring up his powers; but he did long in vain.
> Who then persuaded you to stay at home? (10–15)

Her speech is a reminder, in a very different key, of Falstaff's cynical reflections on the pointlessness of honour at the end of *1 Henry IV* (see Chapter 2 above). The tone of the two scenes could not be more different, but there is an equivalence about their function: to puncture the progress of war and the honour-code that underpins it with an awareness of its devastation, its defeats, and the potential hollowness even of its victories.

This scene reminding us of the continuation of Lady Percy's grief from play to play is unusual in its quiet tone and restrained bodily movement. Grief in the earlier history plays, as suggested by the scene from *Richard III* examined above, is more commonly expressed in high rhetoric or in the shriller register of raving and tearing of hair (as when Constance hears that her son Arthur is John's prisoner in *King John* (3.4)). Indeed, women's functions on stage in the early histories are characteristically more excessive and emotional than in the later plays, where their presence is generally quieter, though it may also be assertive to a degree, as Lady Percy is in this scene. Lady Percy's name, Kate, is one that Shakespeare seems to have characteristically associated with assertiveness or spiritedness, beginning with Katerina in *The Taming of the Shrew*, addressed as Kate by her husband and family. Some of the Kates he presents in the history plays were of course historically named Katherine or its French or Spanish equivalent (as with Catherine de Valois in *Henry V* or Katherine of Aragon in *Henry VIII*), but Lady Percy's historical name was Elizabeth, and Shakespeare changed it to Kate.[7] The repeated use of her name in Act 2, scene 3 of *1 Henry IV* highlights how importantly the recurrence of a personal name in dialogue can shape the scene. It is a scene full of teasing intimacy and affection which, like the grieving scene of *2 Henry IV*, reminds the audience of the world that war intrudes upon and can so easily blow away, the world where husbands and wives, fathers and daughters, mothers and sons, may express their care for one another in the small details and activities of domestic life.

The active use of a name in dialogue can also bring a momentary domesticity, a reminder of personal affection, into scenes that are very different in kind. When Katherine of Aragon sweeps out of the court in the trial scene of *Henry VIII*, Henry's response, 'Go thy ways, Kate' (2.4.130), shoots a reminiscence of their thirty years of intimacy together through the pomp and circumstance of this hitherto very formal scene, changing the impact of the scene briefly but very significantly. Where the distance between them seemed proper to the formality of a trial, it now seems bleak and sad, an improper distance between a close married couple. Henry V similarly domesticates what begins as a formal scene by changing his address to the French princess from Catherine to Kate. He begins with 'Fair Catherine' and a relatively distant form of address ('Will you vouchsafe to teach a soldier terms | Such as will enter at a lady's ear | And plead his love-suit to her gentle heart' (*Henry V*, 5.2.99–101)), terms which imply some physical distance between them on stage at this point. But as his address shifts to 'Do you like me, Kate' (106–7), so it is likely that their positions shift too and Henry moves closer to the Princess. With that shift the formal negotiation of a marriage contract between a victorious and a defeated nation becomes instead, this scene seeks to show, the wooing of a woman by a man who is developing a genuine affection for her:

Yet I love thee, too. And while thou livest, dear Kate, take a fellow of plain and uncoined constancy, for he perforce must do thee right, because he hath not the gift to woo in other places. (151–3)

The name resounds through every one of Henry's speeches here, setting up an image of bluff and plain Englishness against the sophistication and incomprehension of Catherine's French. And this image of simple straightforwardness is likely to be conveyed physically through an increasing closeness, moving towards touch. Quite where the first touch comes is a matter of nuance for the actor, but come it does, since the exchange culminates in a kiss. Catherine's protest (in French) that French maids do not kiss before they are married is silenced with a plethora of 'Kates', doubtless accompanied by continuing physical proximity and touch:

O Kate, nice customs curtsy to great kings. Dear Kate, you and I cannot be confined within the weak list of a country's fashion. We are the makers of manners, Kate . . . You have witchcraft in your lips, Kate. (260–7)

Wooing scenes generally constitute one of the largest groups of domestic scenes in the history plays, though they may be so barbed with irony or deceit as to be virtual parodies of domestic quietude, and not so much interludes in political life as active agents of it. Richard of Gloucester's two wooing scenes, for example (*Richard III*, 1.2 and 4.4), are entirely based on the premiss that the personal interaction between himself and the woman is false, with the pretence of love entirely manufactured for the purpose of furthering Richard's political advancement or stability; and both are Shakespeare's additions to the chronicle sources. The stichomythic patterns of dialogue in each scene seem to highlight the 'stagy' and manufactured nature of the interaction, and the way the second scene imitates the first makes that artfulness even more visible and audible. The dialogue is at first working in tension with the body language of the scene, since Richard's bald statement of purpose is written to suggest shock tactics:

LADY ANNE And thou unfit for any place but hell.
RICHARD DUKE OF GLOUCESTER Yes, one place else, if you will hear me name it.
LADY ANNE Some dungeon.
RICHARD DUKE OF GLOUCESTER Your bedchamber. (1.2.107–9)

If he also moves closer to Anne at this point, the effect is very different from the growing proximity between Henry V and Princess Catherine above, coldly calculating and sinister, rather than warm and light. As he moves closer to press his suit, Anne spits at him, thus highlighting for the audience the hatefulness of his proximity to her.

Yet when he kneels before her, lays open his breast, and presents her with his sword to drive through it, the physical posture does the work that his words alone have been unable to do. As Anne lets fall the sword and bids Richard rise, she is effectively capitulating to his wooing (see Chapter 5 above). Despite her denial she allows him to touch her as he places his ring upon her finger. Though she protests weakly that 'To take is not to give', Richard makes the equation between body and heart in his reply:

> Look how this ring encompasseth thy finger,
> Even so thy breast encloseth my poor heart.
> Wear both of them, for both of them are thine. (189–91)

The sequence of tableaux tells the story of the scene.

As the first wooing scene culminates in Richard's gift to Anne of his ring, so the second culminates in Richard's kiss, to be sent by proxy to Princess Elizabeth via her mother, Richard's sister-in law. But where the first scene ended with Richard's prolonged crowing over his success:

> Was ever woman in this humour wooed?
> Was ever woman in this humour won?
>
> . . .
>
> Shine out, fair sun—till I have bought a glass—
> That I may see my shadow as I pass.[8] (1.2.213–48)

the second action closes with a single line of contempt: 'Relenting fool, and shallow, changing woman' (4.4.350). The difference signals a difference that Richard is at this point ironically unaware of, namely that this second wooing has in fact failed. Queen Elizabeth has no intention of giving him her daughter in marriage and it is she who is in control of the artfulness of this interaction.[9]

The wooing scene reaches a different kind of nadir in *Henry VIII*, when Henry first meets Anne Boleyn. Henry's only motivation for wanting Anne is sexual desire. She is not part of any political agenda on his part, and is in fact to become his greatest political setback. Indeed he has no wish to marry her at all at this point, and wants her only as his mistress. Since she is, of course, as Shakespeare's audiences would have known all too well, eventually to become his wife, this 'wooing' is uneasily situated between mere sexual invitation and the beginning of an all-consuming love. The scene is set, prior to Henry's entry, with a banquet that makes a point of seating men between women as a way of avoiding the 'cold weather' constituted by '[t]wo women placed together' (*Henry VIII*, 1.4.22). This seating arrangement leads directly into the opportunity for some fairly explicit flirtation and heightened proximity. Lord Sands, seated next to Anne Boleyn, freely kisses her within seconds of sitting down next to her. The action is too swift and too close, and signposts the way to the development of the scene. As the drinking and merry-making continue, their conversation becomes more risqué, with open word-play between them on the word 'thing' (a common euphemism for the male sexual organ):

> ANNE   You are a merry gamester,
>   My lord Sands.
> SANDS   Yes, if I make my play.
>   Here's to your ladyship; and pledge it, madam,
>   For 'tis to such a thing—
> ANNE   You cannot show me. (46–9)

The King's first words on seeing Anne briefly take the discourse into a different register, that of idealized wooing: 'The fairest hand I ever touched. O beauty, | Till now I never knew thee' (76–7). The lines echo Tamburlaine's extensive praise of beauty on first sight of Zenocrate, but they cannot and do not neutralize the lewdness that has preceded this encounter; and something of that lewdness returns as Henry asks who Anne is and responds with a change of tone that is considerably more casually and sexually predatory than his first remark: 'By heaven, she is a dainty one' (94).[10] The gaze has changed from admiring love to lip-smacking desire. Henry's language precisely echoes Lord Sands's salacious remarks about the female charms on offer earlier in the scene (13–18), and his use of the dance as an excuse to kiss Anne suggests the same sexual opportunism that Sands showed on first sitting down beside her. Wolsey's eagerness to move the King on and away from the dancing confirms for the audience the sense that this scene is more about lust than love:

> CARDINAL WOLSEY   Your grace,
>   I fear, with dancing is a little heated.
> KING HENRY I fear too much.

CARDINAL WOLSEY   There's fresher air, my lord,
In the next chamber. (102–5)

Side by side, Henry and Anne go off to drink and dance more, as
Henry's closing invitation ('Sweet partner, | I must not yet forsake
you' (107–8)) indicates. The momentary impression of a great love
taking root in Henry's first sight of Anne is reduced by the end of
the scene to overheated desire. Anne is scripted to be silent with the
King, but her active engagement with Sands has already signalled to
the audience that this is no passive, blushing maid.

Wooing scenes in the history plays, then, generally have an agenda
that is very different from wooing scenes in Shakespeare's comedies
and tragedies. Where Juliet, despite her youth, may be less blushing
and more knowing than, say, Hero in *Much Ado About Nothing*, and
Beatrice in *Much Ado* is older and more knowing than either, none is
portrayed as so sexually explicit as Anne is here, and no wooing
between lovers is so wholly and deliberately evacuated of romance
as is this one between Henry and Anne, or so manipulative and
fraudulent as Richard's wooing of his chosen political partners. Of
those discussed here, only Henry V's wooing of Catherine de Valois
emerges as relatively untarnished, and even that is part of a political
agenda, since marriage is the necessary and appropriate way to seal
the peace at the end of the Anglo-French wars. Wooing in the history
plays is usually linked to political movement or, in the case of *Henry
VIII*, a seismic shift in European history. Though it may on occasion
incorporate a personal dimension, that is not its *raison d'être*.

More likely to include private moments and affectionate interaction than wooing scenes are leave-taking scenes; and these are often
scripted to show a more private and physically uninhibited side of the
characters involved. The scene from *2 Henry IV* discussed above
where Lady Percy expresses her feelings about her late husband and
her father-in-law (Act 2, scene 3) is a scene of leave-taking, and, like
so many leave-takings in the history plays, it is a leave-taking preceding a departure to war. So too is Act 2, scene 3 of *1 Henry IV*, where
the teasing but intense affection between Hotspur and his Kate is
revealed. And placed again at a very similar point in different plays
are the Queen's expression of grief at parting with Richard II (*Richard
II*, 2.2) and the leave-taking between Humphrey, Duke of Gloucester,
and his Duchess, Eleanor (*2 Henry VI*, 2.4).[11] The scene with

Richard's Queen is very brief and somewhat formal, since Richard is not present, and Isabella is only reporting her grief to Richard's favourites, Bushy and Bagot. There is thus no opportunity for displaying physical closeness or intimacy. Its function is to point up the 'unborn sorrow, ripe in fortune's womb' (10) of which her grief is harbinger (that is, Richard's political fall), not to present an informal perspective on her relationship with her husband. The only domestic interaction in this play to show a real intimacy between the characters concerned is the scene where the Duchess of York seeks pardon from Bolingbroke, her nephew, for her son's treason. Here the Duchess falls to her knees and will not rise until she has the pardon she seeks. The degree to which personal ties can transform the usual public modes of interaction between aristocratic families is self-evident. Despite the visible embarrassment of both Bolingbroke and York, the Duchess's husband, at what seems to them her excessive, even abject, display of emotion, her love for her son is so great that it overwhelms all protocols of normal polite behaviour. The result is that she gains the pardon she will not rise or leave without.

The leave-taking scene between the Duke and Duchess of Gloucester in *2 Henry VI* is very revealing, and truly shows a side of their relationship and of their individual characters which is not demonstrated in any interaction outside their marriage. Their closeness as a couple is already demonstrated to a degree in the earlier scene where Humphrey tells his wife of his prophetic dream (1.2; see Chapter 5 above). As with Hotspur and Kate, his repeated use of a diminutive pet name ('O Nell, sweet Nell, if thou dost love thy lord' (1.2.17)) reveals his affection for her in that scene; but when she is banished from the kingdom following her treasonous consultation with witches and conjurors, the affection between them is displayed at its most piercing and vulnerable. The proud Duchess is already reduced to humility by her dress and position, since part of her punishment in addition to banishment is to do penance '*barefoot, with a white sheet about her, written verses pinned on her back, and a wax taper burning in her hand*' (2.4.17). Physical abjection is thus imposed upon her, rather than willingly embraced, as by the Duchess of York above. Mortified as she is by the shame of this penance, and its enforced display of the body's vulnerability, Eleanor is concerned for her husband: 'Ah, Gloucester, hide thee from their hateful looks, | And in thy closet pent up, rue my shame' (2.4.24–5). The physical gap between them here may be close, given the emphasis on their mutual love and concern, or it may be more awkwardly distant, given Eleanor's shame at her own abjection. Humphrey may be more inclined towards touch than Eleanor, since his own feelings are of love and compassion, again expressed through the diminutive form of Eleanor's name: 'Be patient, gentle Nell, forget this grief' (27); and Eleanor shifts from 'Gloucester' to the more intimate 'Humphrey' as her bitterness overwhelms her: 'Ah Humphrey, can I bear this shameful yoke?' (38). They circle round the same subjects. She repeats her fears for him and urges him to flee from his enemies, and he repeats his advice that 'Thy greatest help is quiet, gentle Nell' (68). He entreats those who escort her to treat her well and not to let her penance exceed the King's commission. As he turns to go, the final exchange between himself and his wife conveys the intensity of feeling:

> DUCHESS ELEANOR What, gone, my lord, and bid me not farewell?
> DUKE HUMPHREY Witness my tears, I cannot stay to speak.
> *Exeunt Duke Humphrey and his men.*
> DUCHESS ELEANOR Art thou gone too? All comfort go with thee,
> For none abides with me. (86–9)

Humphrey's physical body, like Eleanor's, finally shames him and puts an end to this uneasy farewell. But his departure leaves Eleanor's body momentarily lonely and exposed in the fullness of her shame on stage before she is led off.

Most of the scenes above, like most of the scenes discussed in Chapter 2, are Shakespeare's own creations, additions to the source material that shed a different light on the political events they punctuate from the harsh light of public or ceremonial space. Even though some of them, as shown above, have their own political agendas to pursue, their function is additionally to humanize the figures of history and to set wars, alliances, and dynastic marriages within a context that shows how things might have been different. They suggest the multiple ways in which history is made by individuals with particular feelings in particular places at particular times. Had each felt differently about someone with whom they shared a personal relationship, or acted differently in relation to them, or moved closer to or further away from them, the whole trajectory of history might have moved to different measures.

Close-ups

'Close-up' is a term from film, describing the work of a camera in focusing in at close range, often on a face, so that the surrounding picture is removed. In theatre, very importantly, the bigger picture never disappears. It is always present on stage, and an audience never loses the option to look at the whole stage. Yet there are moments when stagecraft forcefully scripts an intensity of engagement between actor and audience which has similarities to the close-up. The soliloquy is the most common strategy for producing that focus. But what exactly is a soliloquy and how does it function? The word, first recorded by the *OED* in 1604, and never used by Shakespeare, is defined by the *OED* as 'an instance of talking to or conversing with oneself, or of uttering one's thoughts aloud without addressing any person' (sense 1(a)) or 'a literary production representing or imitating a discourse of this nature' (sense 1(b)).[1] In the theatre it is most simply and obviously marked by the solitary body on stage, but it should be noted that a speaker need not by definition be alone when uttering such a speech. Soliloquies are not always spoken by a single actor alone on stage and may occur as asides uttered within surrounding groups of people. Where and how they occur on the stage is important. Do they occur at the start or end of a scene? How are they preceded or followed? How full or otherwise is the stage during and on either side of the soliloquy? How coherent or otherwise are the groupings that frame it? How is the speaker placed in relation to the outgoing, surrounding, or incoming group? What kind of listening, stillness, and silence is scripted for others present? This chapter will seek to address a range of such questions in relation to Shakespeare's history plays.

A number of soliloquies have already been discussed in relation to other subjects in earlier chapters. The Bishop of Winchester's closing soliloquy in the first scene of *1 Henry VI* was discussed in Chapter 1 above, where it was noted that Shakespeare often scripts soliloquies at the end of scenes to reveal or confirm the villainy of a particular character. The soliloquy as a mode of speech in such contexts becomes a figure for the apartness and closed quality of the character who thus hides himself from those on stage but reveals himself to the audience.[2] Physically his apartness is emphasized, as Winchester's is, by a turning aside, and perhaps also a putting of distance between himself and the other actors on stage. The Bastard in *King John*, as noted in Chapter 4 above, closes scenes in soliloquy to very different effect. He too confides in the audience, but what he shares with them at the end of Act 2, scene 1 is not machiavellian scheming but a perspective on the doings of his social superiors that gives the audience a prompt to question the methods and motivations of all concerned. His meditation on commodity offers a clear-sighted, honest look at politics that is not available elsewhere in the play. The position of direct address, probably combined with a position on the perimeter of the stage, close to the audience, is not therefore one that the audience can learn to distrust, since it is the position of honest as well as dishonest characters, and of actors who build relationships of trust with the audience for illuminating and informative as well as dubious purposes.

Later in the same play, the Bastard ends a scene with a soliloquy that produces a further variation on possibilities of interaction with the audience. On this occasion the Bastard, far from seeing things with certainty and clarity as before, is confused and fearful. He has found Arthur dead and Hubert denying all knowledge of his death, though, since Hubert is Arthur's gaoler, suspicion must fall on him. As Hubert lifts Arthur's body, still insisting on his innocence, the Bastard confesses his sense that the whole world about him has become a place of confusion and threat:

> I am amazed, methinks, and lose my way
> Among the thorns and dangers of this world.
> How easy dost thou take all England up! (4.3.140–2)

Despite Hubert's continuing presence on stage, and the direct address to him in line 142, this speech is delivered more to the audience than to Hubert. It is a meditation on the condition of England and the wider consequences of Arthur's death:

> From forth this morsel of dead royalty,
> The life, the right, and truth of all this realm
> Is fled to heaven, and England now is left
> To tug and scramble, and to part by th'teeth
> The unowed interest of proud-swelling state. (143–7)

For an audience, alignment is problematic. They have seen Hubert spare Arthur, and know that he is not guilty of Arthur's death; they have seen the Bastard's instincts proved correct on previous occasions in the play, and know his judgement to be acute; and, while they know his suspicion of Hubert to be misplaced on this occasion, they recognize the truth of his more generalized feeling about England as a moral jungle. They can hear too the shift from soliloquy to direct address in the last few lines of the scene,

> Bear away that child
> And follow me with speed. I'll to the King.
> A thousand businesses are brief in hand,

though the very last line does something different:

> And heaven itself doth frown upon the land. (156–9).

With the reference to the whole land and heaven's judgment of it the perspective shifts again from two men and a dead child to the whole country and its moral state. The effect is similar to a camera widening out its focus at the end of a close-up to show the speaker in a particular time and place. It is, very literally, a moment of truth.

One of the most striking soliloquies in the history plays is the opening of *Richard III*. It is striking partly for the simple reason that it opens the play, a situation unparalleled in Shakespeare's other history plays and indeed remarkable across the whole canon. As John Jowett notes:

At the beginning of *Richard III* the audience first sees an actor alone on stage. He is not a formal prologue who supplies narrative context, but presents a character who is temporarily abstracted from a social world that does not yet exist. Of Shakespeare's major protagonists, Richard is the only one to begin the play addressing the audience.[3]

Unlike the state scenes that open most of the history plays, or the prologues and choruses that open *2 Henry IV, Henry V,* and *Henry VIII,* this opening takes the audience into the world of the play through the single character of Richard, Duke of Gloucester.[4] Though this is the opening of the play, however, many members of a contemporary audience would already know this character from the title of the play, from *2* and *3 Henry VI,* plays that had already been performed in London theatres over the previous two or three years, and from the anonymous Queen's Men's play *The True Tragedy of Richard III.* (Whether there was any continuity between actors and parts across the plays when they were first performed is impossible to resolve.[5]) Those who had seen *3 Henry VI* might remember his soliloquy just before the end of that play, standing over the body of Henry VI, whom he has just murdered. It is an unadulterated confession of unrepentant villainy that seeks to damn the pious Henry to hell; claims to have 'neither pity, love, nor fear'; recalls his mother's story of his being born with teeth to signify that he 'should snarl and bite and play the dog'; and insists on his total apartness from other men:

> I have no brother, I am like no brother,
> And this word 'love' which greybeards call divine,
> Be resident in men like one another
> And not in me: I am myself alone. (5.6.80–3)

For those who had seen the *Henry VI* plays, Richard's association with soliloquy as a mode would also link him to his father, Richard Plantagenet, later Duke of York, and claimant to the throne for the House of York, whose soliloquies begin in *2 Henry VI.*[6] Like Winchester in *1 Henry VI,* Richard of York's machiavellian qualities and isolation are signalled by his soliloquy at the end of the first scene, where he condemns Henry's foolishness in giving away his French lands; chafes against his present need to 'sit and fret and bite his tongue'; and closes the scene with a threatening rhymed couplet:

> And force perforce I'll make him yield the crown,
> Whose bookish rule hath pulled fair England down.
> (*2 Henry VI,* 1.1.229, 257–8)

Opening this new play with a soliloquy was thus a bold move that simultaneously built on prior expectations (the speech and behaviour of Richard of Gloucester and his father in earlier plays—and Gloucester's soliloquy in *3 Henry VI*, 3.2.124–95, the longest soliloquy in any Shakespeare play) and created new ones (what kind of play could this be that began with the central character speaking first, alone, and directly to the audience, a role normally given to the prologue in many older, and some later, plays?).

That opening speech, once so strikingly innovative and surprising, is now so well known as to be almost impossible to hear as if for the first time. At the same time, however, its very over-familiarity sometimes renders it improperly understood. Many listeners, recalling only the opening line, hear it as a louring statement of pure and present discontent: 'Now is the winter of our discontent' (1.1.1); but the continuation of the sentence makes clear that it is actually, at this point, a statement of triumphant satisfaction rather than discontent:

> Now is the winter of our discontent
> Made glorious summer by this sun of York. (1–2)

The clouds that once 'loured upon our house' are now dispersed, the arms of war are 'hung up for monuments', and War (personified) has time to '[caper] nimbly in a lady's chamber' (3–12). Only Richard— and here the transition to discontent begins—is unable to take up the wooing mode of peace because he is deformed; and this deformity, which prevents him from becoming a lover (though he is to become an astoundingly successful wooer in the next scene, as discussed in Chapters 5 and 6 above), is offered to the audience as the motivation for his determination 'to prove a villain' (30). From then on this confidential relationship with the audience becomes Richard's most characteristic mode of acting. Act 1, scene 1 closes with Richard alone, taking the audience into his confidence with regard to his plans again, and ending on the usual rhyming couplet; Act 1, scene 2, following the wooing of Anne, does the same; Act 1, scene 3 moves into soliloquy just before the close of the scene, and is astonishingly direct with the audience about Richard's techniques for gulling others:

> But then I sigh, and with a piece of scripture
> Tell them that God bids us do good for evil.

> And thus I clothe my naked villainy
> With old odd ends stol'n out of holy writ,
> And seem a saint when most I play the devil. (1.3.334–8)

Similar insights are offered later as brief asides rather than extended soliloquies:

> I say, 'Without characters fame lives long.'
> (*Aside*) Thus like the formal Vice Iniquity,
> I moralize two meanings in one word. (3.1.81–3)

The impression given is of a mind buzzing, relentlessly scheming, seeking out and responding to new challenges. As Ron Daniels warned Antony Sher when he took on the part of Richard, it is an exhausting feat of endurance for an actor: 'Hamlet tends to stand there while things happen round him, to him. Richard is doing, doing all the time, making everything happen.'[7] Yet both these very different figures, Hamlet and Richard III, find their characteristic expressive mode to be that of the soliloquy. And the soliloquy can also change in status and effect very considerably over the course of a play. By the time Richard comes to speak his last soliloquy, following the appearance to him in Act 5, scene 4 of the ghosts of all his victims, its dominant mode is fear. The very rhythm of his lines shows a clear disintegration from the smooth confidence of flowing blank verse to the jerky fragmentation of disrupted iambics:

> What do I fear? Myself? There's none else by.
> Richard loves Richard; that is, I am I.
> Is there a murderer here? No.—Yes, I am.
> Then fly.—What, from myself?—Great reason why:
> Lest I revenge.—What, myself upon myself?
> Alack, I love myself.[8] (5.4.161–6)

The soliloquy, once the embodiment of his confidence and seeming invincibility, uttered by a physically deformed body that nevertheless knew how to fill and dominate the stage, has now become the vehicle for a body oppressed by an unstoppable procession of ghosts, a body that cannot prevent itself from expressing shock and fear in an instinctive physical reaction ('*Richard starteth up out of a dream*', 5.4.155), and that is now reduced to looking and moving this way and that, calling for help from any and every direction ('Give me another horse! Bind up my wounds! | Have mercy, Jesu!' (156–7)), displaying a total loss of that control that had at first been its most dominant and visible quality on stage.

Elsewhere in the history plays, soliloquy can perform in a manner diametrically opposed to its dominant mode of functioning in *Richard III*. Where Richard III is indefatigably active and busy, his soliloquies mostly manifesting his plans for the next tranche of activity, Richard II, a character seemingly equally dominated by soliloquy as a mode of speech, is the most still, reflective, and inward-looking of Shakespeare's kings in the history plays. Not just Richard himself, but the whole play, is as static as *Richard III* is active. As Andrew Gurr comments: 'The play is remarkable in the Shakespearean canon for its lack of movement on stage. Most of the action consists of speeches made under varying degrees of formality.'[9] Despite *seeming* to be as strongly characterized by soliloquy as Richard III, however, Richard II does not actually speak anything that might fall into that category until Act 3; and even then all his speeches except the one spoken in prison in Act 5 are semi-public declarations; that is, he may seem to speak to and about himself within a self-involved, inward-looking discourse, but he is actually addressing those around him. More than any character so far considered, Richard II may make us question the limits of what defines a soliloquy as such and suggest the need for a sharper taxonomy of stage discourse that draws distinctions between different kinds of personal or partly self-directed utterance.

His speech in Act 3, scene 2, is entirely conducted in the first-person plural:

> Let's talk of graves, of worms and epitaphs,
> Make dust our paper, and with rainy eyes
> Write sorrow on the bosom of the earth.
> Let's choose executors and talk of wills—
> . . .
> For God's sake, let us sit upon the ground,
> And tell sad stories of the death of kings; (3.2.141–52)

and ends with a direct address to those around him:

> I live with bread, like you; feel want,
> Taste grief, need friends. Subjected thus,
> How can you say to me I am a king? (171–3)

Yet it is a speech which is certainly uttering private thoughts aloud. What it is doing, paradoxically, as its grammatical plurals emphasize, is taking the whole company inside himself, interpellating them as passive—and necessary—recipients of his private meditations. Unlike Richard III, who uses soliloquy to make a collusive relationship with the audience, out of the sight and hearing of other characters in the play, Richard II seems to make no distinction between private and public space. He assumes the whole public sphere as his private domain; and the egotism of this assumption is as monstrous in its way as the egotism of Richard III's determination to ride roughshod over all others to get what he wants.

Physically, Richard's position on stage separates him from the surrounding company in the most posturing and attention-seeking manner. The speech is prompted by news of the treachery of his favourites, the Earl of Wiltshire, Bushy, Bagot, and Greene, and begins by cutting right through the reports and questions of his courtiers with the order to be silent while he determines the nature of the discourse—which is to be his alone:

> AUMERLE Where is the Duke my father, with his power?
> RICHARD No matter where. Of comfort no man speak.
>   Let's talk of graves . . . (139–41)

The peremptory nature of the command is already characteristic of Richard's behaviour in the play, but the extended meditation of this speech, together with the absurd plea to sit down ('For God's sake, let us sit upon the ground') in the midst of a volatile and dangerous political situation, changing fast with every moment that passes, is truly extraordinary. One might doubt whether Richard is actually scripted to literally sit at this point, but the Bishop of Carlisle's sardonic response in the Quarto text is most plausibly spoken to a king who has indeed sat down:

> My lord, wise men ne'er sit and wail their woes,
> But presently prevent the ways to wail.[10](175–6)

Nothing could more clearly indicate the discomfort, even contempt, Richard creates amongst at least some of his men by sitting down to meditate at this key moment in the action, when they should be planning for the growing power of the rebels. Scroope, who brings the news of treachery that prompts Richard to this show of resignation, resumes the unfinished news of those defecting to the other side after Richard has accepted Carlisle's rebuke and pulled himself together. But, while Richard wallows in self-pity for thirty-five lines, Scroope and the others must stand about like waxworks, rendered helplessly passive by Richard's choice to meditate in the midst of action.

His next soliloquy, in the very next scene, is inserted into a context of even more pressing action. It is the scene where Bolingbroke and the rebels arrive at Flint Castle and Richard appears with his courtiers on the walls to hear Northumberland's message from Bolingbroke (see Chapter 4 above). Like his speech in the previous scene, it simply holds up the surrounding action to meditate, and again the themes are death and the burden of kingship. Again spoken publicly, this speech has no imaginary 'we' at its centre, but rather an insistently dominant 'I' and 'my', emerging out of a brief third-person consideration of himself as 'the king'. When the term 'we' does surface, at line 160, it is a royal 'we', designating Richard alone. As before, there is the same growing unease and embarrassment about this extended self-reflection in public space and at a moment when action is necessary, and this time Richard himself is the first to acknowledge it in speech:

> Well, well, I see
> I talk but idly, and you mock at me. (3.3.169–70)

Northumberland can only agree that Bolingbroke is indeed waiting for him below; but in reporting Richard's response moments later he is more frank in his assessment of the speech he has just heard:

> Sorrow and grief of heart
> Makes him speak fondly [foolishly], like a frantic man. (183–4)

The third soliloquy seems even more private, because, though it is again spoken in public before Bolingbroke and the court in the middle of the formal scene of deposition, it is addressed to a looking glass, which Richard specifically calls for (4.1.255). The inwardness of this meditation could not be more inappropriately positioned and highlighted than it is by this solipsistic gesture, which intensifies the focus of the engagement to an extreme degree. Only in the last soliloquy is Richard finally physically alone on stage; and here, at last, his meditation seems to find an appropriate place, since imprisonment quite properly prompts reflection. More importantly, Richard's reflection has moved on here from self-pity and a morbid obsession with death to a more analytical exploration of his own life and the now very real threat of death. But death now looks like an easeful prospect of nothingness, by comparison with the suffering of life, and there is a certain recognition of justice here which has been absent from his earlier meditations: 'I wasted time, and now doth time waste me' (5.5.49). This is the only occasion on which the audience is positioned to respond directly to Richard II, as he speaks about himself to himself alone, and not as part of a spectacle mounted for public consumption.

The remaining plays of the Second Tetralogy, *1* and *2 Henry IV* and *Henry V*, open up yet another new way of handling soliloquy and a seeming continuity across the development, through soliloquy, of the figure who begins as Prince Hal and becomes Henry V. Scholars disagree as to whether these plays were planned as a sequence, but whether or not they were first conceived in that way, it is certainly the case that as each new play appeared, it built upon the narrative and techniques of those preceding it.[11] This Prince's (or King's) soliloquies are a relatively rare event. There is only one in each play, and it is always spoken alone. The first, in *1 Henry IV*, comes as a surprise, partly because of its nature and content and partly because it is unlike any soliloquy previously encountered in the history plays. It is, as David Bevington writes, totally 'unlike Richard III's chortling confidences or Richard II's meditation on the vanity of human existence [and] leaves us uncertain as to its intent'.[12] It creeps into the play early on, but suddenly and unexpectedly, following a scene of seemingly relaxed and easy playfulness between Hal, Falstaff, and Poins (1.2). The scene is in prose and shows the first interaction between Falstaff and the Prince. They joke with one another and plan a robbery together, clearly not for the first time: 'Where shall we take a purse tomorrow, Jack?' (95), asks Hal. The scene is also full of questions and allusions on Falstaff's part to how life will be when Hal is king. The relationship looks like one of competing wit and affectionate teasing, based on mutual understanding. Towards the end of the scene, however, Poins and the Prince plan a complication of the robbery plot, which involves the two of them, in disguise, robbing Falstaff and his friends after they have performed the first robbery. The idea is Poins's, but Hal's willingness to go along with this plan gives us the first hint that his alliance with Falstaff is not so firm as it may have briefly seemed.

As Poins leaves, the Prince's soliloquy addresses an absent 'you' which comprises all his alehouse friends, including both Falstaff and Poins:

> I know you all, and will awhile uphold
> The unyoked humour of your idleness. (183–4)

Its tone is so suddenly distant, so knowing, and so dismissive as to be shocking. This same young man who moments ago was treating his fellows like equals and deciding that 'once in my days I'll be a madcap' (134) is evidently no madcap. He is, it now becomes clear, not someone who ever, even momentarily, loses control of himself. Instead, his whole way of being with these 'friends' is calculated as a policy to 'imitate the sun', temporarily covered by clouds, so that

> when he please again to be himself
> Being wanted he may be more wondered at
> By breaking through the foul and ugly mists
> Of vapours that did seem to strangle him. (188–91)

His tavern 'friends' are in fact a stratagem for presenting himself to the world as a redeemed character. The plan is simple, but devastating, as the closing rhymed couplet of his soliloquy announces with breathtaking coolness:

> I'll so offend to make offence a skill,
> Redeeming time when men think least I will. (204–5)

The function of the soliloquy has affinities with those of Richard III, in that it reveals to the audience a truth hiding behind a masquerade; but perhaps the most significant difference is that this is, as John Cox puts it, 'not a bad man pretending to be good but a good man pretending to be bad'; with the significant qualification, of course, that the deceitfulness itself is morally very dubious.[13]

The play never returns to present the Prince in soliloquy again. On the contrary, the figure who most often speaks alone on stage is Falstaff, who several times has the last word in a scene, whether that be simply a line or two or an extended commentary. The result of this new dramaturgy is to create a very different kind of effect from the soliloquies of either *Richard III* or *Richard II*, different though those already are from one another. Instead of hearing the soliloquy as the voice of the undeniably central character, the dominant speaker of the play, the audience hears the Prince's voice in this mode once only, in a play that more often cedes this kind of vocal dominance and solitary stage presence to Falstaff. Remaining on stage to speak the closing lines of a scene is a powerful position, one that can seem to give a clinching, summative quality to those final words and which encourages the audience to see the action through the eyes of that closing perspective. Falstaff's speech on honour (discussed in Chapter 2 above) sets the military ambitions of both Hal and Hotspur in a quizzical light; but it is not the only occasion on which Hal's presence and position are sceptically enclosed by Falstaff's. Falstaff's rhyming couplet at the close of Act 4, scene 3, where preparations for battle are becoming urgent, is similarly alienating on the subject of military glory:

> Well, to the latter end of a fray and the beginning of a feast
> Fits a dull fighter and a keen guest, (4.3.75–6)

as is his prose resolution of Act 5, scene 3:

Well, if Percy be alive, I'll pierce him. If he do come in my way, so; if he do not, if I come in his willingly let him make a carbonado [grilled meat] of me. I like not such grinning honour as Sir Walter hath. Give me life, which if I can save, so; if not, honour comes unlooked for, and there's an end. (55–60)

Since honour does indeed come unlooked for for Falstaff in the next scene, where he falsely and brazenly claims the honour of having killed Hotspur, the Prince's quest for honour, and the absence of any soliloquy from him putting this point of view (together with the dubious moral position of his only soliloquy), gives Falstaff's cynical pragmatism considerable force.

Prince Hal's only soliloquy in the next play in sequence, *2 Henry IV*, is placed much later in the play than his soliloquy in *1 Henry IV*. It reverses the dramaturgical strategy of Part One (which placed the Prince's soliloquy early on and then regularly gave Falstaff a concluding role in later scenes) by giving Falstaff the closure of two earlier scenes (1.2 and 3.2) and letting that quasi-dominance cede to

Hal's soliloquy in Act 3, scene 4. Falstaff's closure of Act 3, scene 2, furthermore, ends with a sentiment that could be seen as ventriloquizing for the Prince's coming withdrawal of friendship (which an audience familiar with Part One is anticipating): 'Let time shape, and there an end' (316–17). There is also a further significant point about the placing of Hal's soliloquy in this play, and that is the careful reminder to the audience of his earlier confession of strategy in Part One, given to the Earl of Warwick some 70 lines before Hal is left alone with his father here. The Prince, advises Warwick, 'but studies his companions'. He will:

> in the perfectness of time
> Cast off his followers, and their memory
> Shall as a pattern or a measure live
> By which his grace must mete the lives of other,
> Turning past evils to advantages. (4.3.748)

Not only does this soliloquy remind (or inform) audiences of the content of the Prince's soliloquy in Part One; it also presents that reminder in a positive light, with the Earl of Warwick's seeming approval of the Prince's plan.

The Prince's soliloquy itself, discussed in Chapter 5 above, is more an address to kingship than a piece of self-revelation. Addressing the crown that lies on the pillow beside his sick father's head, he laments the burdens of majesty and contemplates the ambivalent combination of honour and responsibility he must inherit from his father. It is a relatively impersonal speech, somewhat predictable in its content and rather lacking in affect. It is also spoken against a musical accompaniment, which gives it something of the distance and self-enclosure of song, setting it apart from the surrounding action, like an inserted meditation. Like his father, Henry IV (the Bolingbroke of *Richard II*), and like Richard III in as far as his character has obvious parallels with that of his father, Prince Hal is deliberately opaque; but unlike Richard III, he remains opaque to the audience as well as to most of the characters on stage. Warwick's true perception of his motive for spending time with low-life companions in taverns is unique across the three plays in which Hal figures.[14]

There is an even more evident continuity between this soliloquy and Hal's last soliloquy, now as Henry V, in the play of that name.

Like the one in *2 Henry IV*, the soliloquy in *Henry V* is placed relatively late in the play (4.1) and its subject is again the burden of kingship; and like the earlier soliloquy in Part One, it follows on from a scene in company with socially inferior subjects. But this preceding interaction with social inferiors is interestingly different in the two plays. In *1 Henry IV* the Prince mixes easily with his tavern companions in a relationship of quasi-equality and seeming good fellowship, which is not revealed as anything other than that until the Prince's soliloquy discloses that he is using them for his own ends; but in *Henry V* it is the men, not the King, who reveal the element of bad faith in this second attempt to slip under the barriers of social status. As discussed in Chapter 5 above, the King's attempt, disguised as a common soldier, to join a company of men as one of them the night before Agincourt ends up in a quarrel, where the King exchanges gloves with one Williams in token of their mutual determination to finish the quarrel after the battle. The gathering thus breaks up in some bad feeling, and Henry's soliloquy follows as the soldiers leave. He laments the heavy moral responsibility that subjects expect the King to bear and longs for the 'infinite heartsease ... that private men enjoy' (4.1.224–5). Ceremony, he asserts, is the only thing kings have that private men do not, and that is nothing but 'place, degree, and form, | Creating awe and fear in other men' (234–5).

His soliloquy is interrupted by the entry of Sir Thomas Erpingham, bringing warmth into the coldness Henry's encounter with his soldiers has left:

> My lord, your nobles, jealous of your absence,
> Seek through your camp to find you. (273–4)

Perhaps it is this note of care and concern that prompts Henry to resume his soliloquy in a very different mode after Erpingham leaves. He turns from bitterness against his burden and envy of the common man's lot to a prayer that moves from care for his men to an admission of personal, or at least inherited, guilt:

> Not today, O Lord,
> O not today, think not upon the fault
> My father made in compassing the crown. (280–2)

Here, finally, from a king whose soliloquies have concentrated mainly on kingship, is a brief insight into a deeper part of the self, where a real awareness of guilt remains unallayed by all acts of penitence:

> I have built
> Two chantries, where the sad and solemn priests
> Sing still for Richard's soul. More will I do.
> Though all that I can do is nothing worth,
> Since that my penitence comes after ill,
> Imploring pardon. (288–93)

The play never again reveals Henry's tormented soul. It moves forward to the victory of Agincourt, the courtship of the French Princess Catherine (see Chapter 6 above), and the uniting of France and England under Henry V. Only the epilogue reminds the audience that the high point reached at the end of this play gives way to the disastrous losses Shakespeare began by dramatizing in his very first history plays:

> Henry the Sixth, in infant bands crowned king
> Of France and England, did this king succeed,
> Whose state so many had the managing
> That they lost France and made his England bleed,
> Which oft our stage hath shown—and, for their sake,
> In your fair minds let this acceptance take. (Epilogue, 9–14)

The function of the soliloquies and the prayer is in some ways similar to the function of domestic scenes: it is to point up a personal dimension in the lives of those who make history, which in turn helps to problematize the perception of history that the audience forms from the plays.

History and Providence

There are certain moments in soliloquy, as shown in Chapter 7 above, when the speaker goes into quasi-choric mode to comment on the condition of England or the way the world is.[1] Such moments can be seen either as part of the soliloquy or as punctuating it; that is, they can be delivered as though part of a private meditation or as spoken to an audience, whether on or off stage or both. Similarly choric speeches, of a more extensive nature, occur more regularly outside soliloquy, within scenes of ongoing dialogue. Thus, when John of Gaunt is dying and meditating on Richard II's faults, he shifts into a lyrical paean to England:

> This royal throne of kings, this sceptred isle,
> This earth of majesty, this seat of Mars,
> This other Eden, demi-paradise,
> This fortress built by nature for herself
> Against infection and the hand of war,
> This happy breed of men, this little world,
> This precious stone set in the silver sea
> . . .
> This blessed plot, this earth, this realm, this England.
> (*Richard II*, 2.1.40–50)

His speech seems to rise above and supersede the immediate context that has prompted it and to invite both the onstage and the offstage audience to pause in their engagement with the continuing action of the play to consider its significance in the greater scheme of things. The sheer length of the speech, which runs for a total of nearly forty lines, scripts a silent tableau for those around the dying John of Gaunt and makes the fullness of Richard's entry with seven others at line 68 seem disturbing and disruptive to the meditative and universalizing cast of mind that this deathbed speech has produced. Suddenly the daily lives of others, even kings, seem trivial and even futile by comparison with the larger vision that comes with death.

Such moments of pause, which step outside the flow of events to frame them within the wider and longer march of history, owe a debt to the chroniclers who form Shakespeare's sources, and who also pause in the flow of narrative periodically to reflect on the nature and significance of events. John of Gaunt's speech has no direct source at this point in the narratives of Hall or Holinshed, but these two and other Tudor historians insert their own universalizing commentary at different points. Holinshed, for example, offering the opinion that Richard II's errors of conduct 'ought rather to be imputed to the frailty of wanton youth, than to the malice of his heart', moves into a generalizing observation about human error:

such is the deceivable judgement of man, which not regarding things present with due consideration, thinketh ever that things to come shall have good success, with a pleasant and delightful end. But in this dejecting of the one [Richard], and advancing of the other [Bolingbroke], the providence of God is to be respected, and his secret will to be wondered at. For as in his hands standeth the donation of kingdoms, so likewise the disposing of them consisteth in his pleasure.[2]

Hall similarly defers to God's justice in reporting Richard III's last battle:

In the mean season King Richard (which was appointed now to finish his last labour by the very divine justice and providence of God, which called him to condign punishment for his scelerate [deeply wicked] merits and mischievous deserts) marched to a place meet for two battles to encounter by a village called Bosworth not far from Leicester;[3]

and asks rhetorical questions of Henry IV's attempt to secure his title to the throne and his son's succession:

But O Lord, what is the mutability of fortune? O God what is the change of worldly safety? O Christ what stableness consisteth in man's provision? Or what firm surety hath a prince in his throne and degree?[4]

The content of these reflections is entirely different from that of John of Gaunt's speech, but the effect, of taking the reader or spectator out of his or her immersion in the narrative or drama and into a more generalizing mode, is similar. In the play, it is as though the action pauses for the voice of an implicit chronicler to emerge. The words are spoken in a recognizably different register; they seem to be, to use a metaphor from print, italicized.[5]

The fact that God's providence is the subject of Holinshed's meditation quoted above is not random, but of considerable significance for the history plays, which engage repeatedly, and sometimes sceptically, with the question of providence. So too do the chronicle sources, which can also be sceptical on occasion. Hall, for example, citing the apparently supernatural signs of crowns falling down spontaneously at the time of the Duke of York's challenge to the throne in 1460, writes that there was a tendency to interpret these:

as a sign and prognostication, that the crown of the realm should be divided and changed, from one line to another. This was the judgement of the common people, which were neither of God's privity, nor yet of his privy counsel, and yet they will say their opinions, whosoever say nay.

As Nicholas Grene points out, however, Hall's scepticism coexisted alongside his voicing of conventional pieties on the providential shape of the history he was constructing, and chroniclers generally oscillated between a providential and a more naturalistic, Machiavellian point of view.[6]

At the least sceptical end of the spectrum in Shakespeare's history plays are scenes such as Act 5, scene 4 of *Richard III*, where the ghosts of Richard's victims appear to Richard and Richmond in turn (see Chapter 3 above). Scenes with ghosts in them are easily perceived by the audience as different in kind and quality from the surrounding action: ghosts may enter and exit the stage differently, move differently on stage, be marked out by special costuming, deliver their lines in idiosyncratic ways, or maintain a special quality of silence.[7] Such speech as they utter is usually also marked out as different, whether by its paucity and elliptical quality, its formal patterning, or its language (some spirits speak in Latin). There can be no doubt that the ghosts in *Richard III* are scripted to be understood as genuine ghosts. Not only do they appear visibly on stage to the audience and separately to two witnesses, but their curses on Richard and blessings on Richmond come to pass. The formulaic symmetry of their entries and speeches emphasizes the italicizing effect of their words and presence, the way they seem to hold time still; and their appearance on stage just before Richmond's climactic victory of Bosworth and the death of Richard creates a unity of perspective which clearly celebrates Richmond and damns Richard. The point of this scene is to make the audience really pause and take in the significance of this coming battle and change of reigns. The parade of Richard's victims represents a terrible revisiting of the years of chaos and violence that are finally about to give way to the reign of a king who will unite the houses of York and Lancaster.

Like the ghosts in *Richard III*, the fiends that appear on stage to Joan la Pucelle are also to be understood as real spirits, with a separate existence from Joan. Thunder sounds when she summons them to her, and their immediate appearance on stage provides evidence of her witchcraft.[8] As she herself says: 'This speedy and quick appearance argues proof | Of your accustomed diligence to me' (*1 Henry VI*, 5.3.8–9). It is also possible that they rise through the trapdoor, thus confirming their entry from another world. Unlike the ghosts in *Richard III*, however, these spirits do not speak, but use silence to signal their refusal to give Joan any further support: '*They walk and speak not . . . they hang their heads*' (12, 17). This creates a very powerful stage presence for them. Their silent walking and refusal to acknowledge Joan's pleas for help to conquer England reduce her to ever more extreme offers of sacrifice, all further condemning her, within the discourse of the period, as a witch. Referring to her previous practice of feeding them with her blood (one of the known indicators of witchcraft), she first offers to lop off a limb; and when they shake their heads in refusal of this offer, she further offers her soul; at which point they simply depart. The effect is of a very forceful otherworldly presence on stage, its silent stillness framing the frantic speech and gestures of La Pucelle as foolish and futile. The fact that they are evil (a point made partly by the stage direction that refers to them as '*fiends*' (6) and partly by the textual references to them as 'familiar spirits' (10), fed by her blood) makes their departure from her even more ominous. To be deserted even by evil spirits is to have reached the end-point of life and to face death and damnation. It is Joan herself who speaks the closing prophecy that pinpoints and holds still the significance of this scene:

> My ancient incantations are too weak,
> And hell too strong for me to buckle with.
> Now, France, thy glory droopeth to the dust. (27–9)

Not all spirits that appear visibly on stage have such a clear independent existence, however, nor are all ghostly utterances so monologically presented as self-evident truth as they are in *Richard III*. The Spirit that appears in Act 1, scene 4 of *2 Henry VI* is as visible to both the audience and all present on stage as any of the spirits discussed in *Richard III* or *1 Henry VI* above, yet it is summoned by charlatans who plan their strategy in advance, sounding very much like fakes: 'Mother Jourdayne, be you prostrate and grovel on the earth' (11–12). The conjuring ceremonies take the form of invoking and questioning the Spirit, who answers with only riddling truth.[9] In answering the question of what the King's fate shall be, for example, its grammar allows two contradictory interpretations:

> The Duke yet lives that Henry shall depose,
> But him outlive and die a violent death;[10](29–30)

and other answers have a similar slipperiness about them. The material presence of the Spirit and the plausibility of its answers thus partly encourages an audience to believe that this is the authentic voice of a world beyond the everyday pronouncing on the shape of things to come; but at the same time the tricksiness of both the prophecies and those doing the conjuring encourages scepticism. And this position is prepared for in the earlier scene where Sir John Hum, an associate of the Conjuror and the Witch, tells the audience in soliloquy that he has been hired by Cardinal Beaufort and the Duke of Suffolk to entrap the Duchess.

Conjuring and witchcraft were crimes punishable by death in Elizabethan England. The Act against Conjurations Enchantments and Witchcrafts (1563) stated that: 'if any person or persons . . . use practise or exercise any invocations or conjurations of evil and wicked spirits to or for any intent or purpose; or . . . if any person or persons . . . shall use practise or exercise any witchcraft enchantment charm or sorcery whereby any person shall happen to be killed or destroyed', such persons, if found guilty, would be condemned to death.[11] This statute suggests the survival of a belief in witchcraft and the conjuration of spirits, despite the gradual and simultaneous emergence of a scepticism that would eventually become dominant.[12] Shakespeare is willing to make use of either belief system to make different points in particular plays. Thus, while the fiends in *1 Henry VI* confirm the status of Joan la Pucelle as a witch for an early modern English audience already inclined to condemn her as such, the conjuration of spirits in *2 Henry VI* is used instead to demonstrate the manipulation of popular belief by political realists who know better; and the different kind of presence these different spirits have on stage is part of those opposing strategies. The fiends in *1 Henry VI* have a gravitas and a centred intensity of focus that is scripted through their silence and their controlled and restrained gestures and movements; but the appearance of the Spirit in *2 Henry VI* is framed as less intense by the view behind the scenes that precedes it and the presence of two kinds of audience on stage, the conjuring group that know themselves to be manipulating the appearance of this Spirit for political ends, and the credulous Duchess, watching the show from the gallery above, accompanied by one of the charlatans ('it shall be convenient, Master Hum, that you be by her aloft, while we be busy below', instructs Roger Bolingbroke, the conjuror (1.4.7–9)). The performance of the conjuration ceremonies on stage then begins to shift towards an uncertain intensity of focus, putting the audience in a very unclear position, where they know that these people are fakes, but also see them perform forbidden practices that appear to produce a genuine result: '*Here they do the ceremonies belonging, and make the circle. South-well reads 'Coniuro te', etc. It thunders and lightens terribly, then the spirit riseth*' (22). For any audience members that had seen Marlowe's *Dr Faustus* (probably first performed in 1588–9) the scene would be strongly reminiscent of the very intense scene in which Faustus conjures up Mephistopheles, a scene which was later to be represented on the title page of the printed play.[13]

Elizabethan and earlier statutes also forbade the use of prophecy, which could be a powerful weapon for destabilizing the status and safety of the reign.[14] Prophecies for the succession of the monarch, for example, could be a way of fomenting political unrest by manipulating popular opposition to the current regime. Shakespeare uses prophecies and curses throughout the early history plays as another way of moving outside the frame of events into commentary or metanarrative. The end-point of political unity in the person of Henry VII at the close of *Richard III*, for example, has already been strikingly signalled in *3 Henry VI*. Shakespeare gives a notable prophetic cast and intensity of focus to a chance meeting between Henry VI, briefly restored to the throne at this point, and the young Earl of Richmond:

> HENRY My lord of Somerset, what youth is that
>   Of whom you seem to have so tender care?
> SOMERSET My liege it is young Henry, Earl of Richmond.
> HENRY Come hither England's hope.
>   *Lays his hand on Richmond's head*
>   If secret powers
>   Suggest but truth to my divining thoughts,
>   This pretty lad will prove our country's bliss.
>   His looks are full of peaceful majesty,
>   His head by nature framed to wear a crown,
>   His hand to wield a sceptre, and himself
>   Likely in time to bless a regal throne.
>   Make much of him, my lords, for this is he
>   Must help you more than you are hurt by me. (4.6.65–76)

Shakespeare did not invent this scene. Hall and Holinshed both recount Henry VI seeing the future Henry VII as a child at this point and commenting: 'Lo, surely this is he, to whom both we and our adversaries leaving the possession of all things, shall hereafter give room and place'; and both chroniclers, having given Henry VI this prophetic moment, go on to endorse his prophecy as part of a providential framework they themselves wish to underline: 'So this holy man showed before, the chance that should happen, that this earl Henry so ordained by God, should in time to come (as he did indeed) have and enjoy the kingdom, and the whole rule of the realm.'[15] Shakespeare, by way of emphasizing the increased holiness of Henry VI before he utters this prophecy, has him hand over the government of England to Warwick and Clarence as joint Protectors, while he himself plans to:

> lead a private life
> And in devotion spend my latter days
> To sin's rebuke and my creator's praise; (4.6.42–4)

and this prepares the way for a saintly aura to frame his later prophecy, so that both the speaking of it and the listening to it attain a special still quality on stage.

The child Richmond has stood silently on stage, unannounced and unidentified, up to this point. His presence may have attracted curiosity in the audience, and there may be some expectation surrounding him by the time Henry turns his attention to him and asks his name. The gesture scripted for Henry, to lay his hand on Richmond's head, creates a tableau of holiness that brings the piety of Henry VI together with the providential role of Henry VII. Besides being the traditional gesture of blessing, it is also a gesture that recalls the ceremonial laying on of hands in holy rituals such as the ordination of priests and the coronation of kings (where the laying on of hands takes the form of anointing the new king's body). It seals an important link between Henry VI and Henry VII that suggests the willing transfer of kingship from the one to the other.[16] The length of Henry VI's blessing here has the effect of holding the tableau still for a significant length of time and deepening the intensity of the audience's engagement with it. Henry VI's speech of blessing and Henry VII's silent presence come together to create a powerfully dramatic moment that is the theatrical equivalent of the chroniclers' explicit intervention to confirm that Henry VII was ordained by God. Like the appearance of ghosts, it creates the space for the audience to feel the fleeting presence of another world, a world where divine justice shapes the outcome of events in this world of seeming disorder.

Prophecies shape the whole sequence of the First Tetralogy, each prophecy creating its own brief moment of reflection out of time and on the times. Warwick, towards the end of the Temple Garden scene in *1 Henry VI* (see Chapter 3 above), says, as he chooses the white rose of York:

> And here I prophesy: this brawl today,
> Grown to this faction in the Temple garden,
> Shall send between the red rose and the white
> A thousand souls to death and deadly night. (2.4.124–7)

Exeter, alone on stage at the end of Act 4, scene 1 of the same play, closes the scene with similarly prophetic words:

> 'Tis much when sceptres are in children's hands,
> But more when envy breeds unkind division—
> There comes the ruin; there begins confusion. (192–4)

And curses have a similar capacity to freeze the moment for wider contemplation. Margaret is the prime voice of curse in these early histories, so much so that Queen Elizabeth asks her to teach her how to curse (see Chapter 6 above). Margaret's appalling catalogue of curses in the first act of *Richard III* is both climactic, in terms of its retrospective summary of the violence of the preceding plays, and ominous, in terms of the hideous vengeance it calls down for the future on a wide range of those standing by: Queen Elizabeth, Rivers, Dorset, Hastings, and Richard of Gloucester, the future Richard III. Its sheer length, together with its formal matching of each curse to the crimes committed, gives it the universalizing status of prophecy or otherworldliness, as does the address to heaven that precedes the curses themselves:

> Can curses pierce the clouds and enter heaven?
> Why then, give way, dull clouds, to my quick curses. (1.3.192–3)

Even more hideous than this perhaps is the curse of a mother, which steps out of time in Act 4, scene 4, to look ahead to Richard's defeat and death:

> Therefore take with thee my most heavy curse,
> Which in the day of battle tire thee more
> Than all the complete armour that thou wear'st.
> My prayers on the adverse party fight,
> And there the little souls of Edward's children
> Whisper the spirits of thine enemies,
> And promise them success and victory.
> Bloody thou art, bloody will be thy end.
> Shame serves thy life, and doth thy death attend.
> *Exit.* (177–85)

The concluding rhyme and the Duchess's exit give added prominence, closure, and completeness to this prophetic curse.

Yet Shakespeare's history plays do not always adopt such a rever-ential or fearful stance towards prophecy. When the prophet Peter of Pomfret in *King John* prophesies that 'ere the next Ascension Day at noon, | Your highness should deliver up your crown' (4.2.151–2), his prophecy proves true only in the very banal sense that John hands over his crown to the Papal Legate, Cardinal Pandulph, and receives it back again immediately.[17] More pointedly, the later history plays dispense with prophecies and curses almost completely, and give Warwick these shrewdly realistic lines about the status of prophecy:

> There is a history in all men's lives
> Figuring the natures of the times deceased;
> The which observed, a man may prophesy,
> With a near aim, of the main chance of things
> As yet not come to life, who in their seeds
> And weak beginnings lie entreasured. (*2 Henry IV*, 3.1.79–84)

Close observation and an analytical cast of mind, in other words, may produce an accurate forecast of events to come. Or, to put it another way, the study of history is the best way to predict the future. Owen Glendower, who claims to be able to 'call spirits from the vasty deep', becomes the object of Hotspur's mockery in *1 Henry IV*:

> Why so can I, or so can any man;
> But will they come when you do call for them? (3.1.52–3)

And when he goes on to insist that he can command the devil, Hotspur challenges him 'to shame the devil | By telling truth' (55–6). The hard-headed realism of these later history plays makes very little space for moments of aura. Indeed the closest they come to creating a mythologizing or universalizing moment that seems to hold up the narrative in order to step out of time is the Hostess's account of the death of Falstaff:

Nay, sure he's not in hell. He's in Arthur's bosom. A made a finer end, and went away an it had been any christom child. A parted ev'n just between twelve and one, ev'n at the turning o'th' tide—for after I saw him fumble with the sheets, and play with flowers, and smile upon his finger's end, I knew there was but one way. For his nose was as sharp as a pen, and a babbled of green fields. 'How now, Sir John?' quoth I. 'What, man! Be o' good cheer.' So a cried out, 'God, God, God', three or four times. Now I, to comfort him, bid him a should not think of God: I hoped there was no need to trouble himself with any such thoughts yet. So a bade me lay more clothes on his feet. I put my hand into the bed and felt them, and they were as cold as any stone. Then I felt to his knees, and so up'ard and up'ard, and all was cold as any stone. (*Henry V*, 2.3.9–24)

The speech is full of circumstantial and material detail, interspersed with reported dialogue and comically resistant to the idea of God; yet its length, its rhetorical repetitions, and its intensity of focus all tend towards instating it as the mythologizing of a great comic figure (a mythologizing that helps to counter and problematize any tendency to mythologize Henry V himself).[18]

Shakespeare's last history play, *Henry VIII*, brings together the sceptical and the mythologizing casts of mind in the most intriguing way, creating a very uncertain position for the spectator. It is full of quasi-prophetic statements that have no mythologizing or universalizing aura about them at all; yet it includes a vision and a prophecy which are two of the most markedly significant in all the history plays. Characters repeatedly foresee the obvious, in much the way that Warwick suggests in *2 Henry IV*. Buckingham, arrested for high treason in the first scene of the play, foresees his approaching fall:

> My life is spanned already.
> I am the shadow of poor Buckingham,
> Whose figure even this instant cloud puts on
> By dark'ning my clear sun. (1.1.224–7)

The worldly-wise Old Lady foresees Anne Boleyn's rise to the ranks of Duchess and Queen (2.3). Wolsey, like Buckingham, sees the King's anger and knows what must follow:

> I have touched the highest point of all my greatness,
> And from that full meridian of my glory
> I haste now to my setting. I shall fall
> Like a bright exhalation in the evening,
> And no man see me more. (3.2.224–8)

Suffolk, caught with others of the Council scheming to bring Cranmer down, reminds the rest that:

> I told ye all,
> When we first put this dangerous stone a-rolling,
> 'Twould fall upon ourselves. (5.2.137–9)

Yet this same play incorporates the astoundingly sacralized scene of Queen Katherine's vision. Its staging sets it notably apart from the rest of the play. First, it is very sedentary. Katherine asks for a chair because she is 'sick to death' (4.2.1), and audiences would already be very familiar with the stage convention of the sick-chair.[19] Not only did sitting or being carried in a chair regularly signal sickness, but it was very often also a sign of the final stage of sickness before death. Dying characters, furthermore, often have universal wisdom to deliver. John of Gaunt, as we have seen, delivers his speech on England at the point of death (and probably, on the early modern stage, from a sick-chair), and Edmund Mortimer, in a sick-chair at the point of death, summarizes and justifies the York claim to the throne to his heir, Richard Plantagenet (*1 Henry VI*, 2.5.63–97). The first part of the scene of Katherine's vision shows Griffith, her gentleman-usher, recounting the death of Wolsey, and this account of death, together with the kindness of Griffith and Katherine, prepares the way for Katherine's own death. There is then a step-change in the scene at the point where Katherine calls for music:

> Cause the musicians play me that sad note
> I named my knell, whilst I sit meditating
> On that celestial harmony I go to.
> *Sad and solemn music.* (78–80)

This speech, taken together with the sick-chair and the music itself, are unmistakable signs of impending death, and also provide very clear directions for staging: music, stillness, a seated posture for Katherine, and quiet contemplation. Griffith's address to Patience, Katherine's allegorically named lady-in-waiting, confirms the same position of quiet stillness for the two of them:

> She is asleep. Good wench, let's sit down quiet
> For fear we wake her. Softly, gentle Patience. (81–2)

There follows an extraordinarily detailed stage direction scripting a vision for which there is no equivalent in the chronicles, though there are several parallels in Shakespeare's other late plays:

Enter, solemnly tripping one after another, six personages clad in white robes, wearing on their heads garlands of bays and golden visors on their faces. They carry branches of bays or palm in their hands. They first congé [bow] unto Katherine, then dance; and, at certain changes, the first two hold a spare garland over her head, at which the other four make reverent curtsies. Then the two that held the garland deliver the same to the other next two, who observe the same order in their changes and holding the garland over her head. Which done, they deliver the same garland to the last two, who likewise observe the same order. At which, as it were by inspiration, she makes in her sleep signs of rejoicing and holdeth up her hands to heaven. And so in their dancing vanish, carrying the garland with them. The music continues.[20]

Here, then, the stillness of Katherine and her attendants is not there to make the space for prophecy or even magic, but for religious blessing, expressed through dance. This is no less than the apotheosis of Queen Katherine. It is quite remarkable for its time and place, in a post-Reformation play that will end by celebrating the future Queen Elizabeth, daughter of Anne Boleyn, the wife for whom Henry VIII casts off Katherine. In Shakespeare's other late plays, the parallel moments of transformation or revelation are set in fantasized settings such as ancient times, distant lands, or an enchanted island; and the transformations, though they may be magical or quasi-magical, have no topical religious meaning. But this play, performed in the reign of King James and possibly in his presence, creates here a scene that steps aside from the secular narrative into the realm of eternity by presenting the celestial joy that will welcome Henry VIII's discarded Queen at the point of death.

Set against that, yet with no explicit flagging up of any conflict between the two moments, is the play's closing prophecy for Elizabeth, child of the marriage that caused both Katherine of Aragon's personal tragedy and the break with Rome. Archbishop Cranmer's speech of prophecy is as extreme in its celebration of this Queen and her successor, King James, as Katherine's vision was in its celebration of her:

> She shall be—
> But few now living can behold that goodness—
> A pattern to all princes living with her,
> And all that shall succeed.
> . . .
> So shall she leave her blessedness to one,
> When heaven shall call her from this cloud of darkness,
> Who from the sacred ashes of her honour

> Shall star-like rise as great in fame as she was,
> And so stand fixed.
>
> . . .
>
> Our children's children
> Shall see this and bless heaven. (5.4.20–55)

The stage is full for Cranmer's prophecy, following the extended processional entry of the whole court for the child's christening; and all stand still and rapt on stage as Cranmer delivers this lengthy speech. Only Henry's thanks and the epilogue follow. Despite all the cynical and knowing moments about the actions and motivations of the great in this play about relatively recent history, it nevertheless presents these two points of unqualified rapture, stepping out of time to look forward on the one hand to a blessed death and on the other to a reign of perfect grace. No other Shakespearian history play ends with anything like such rejoicing. Yet its view of history seems to combine scepticism with providence, as well as conflicting views of providence itself.

The Power of the State

Chapter 1 began with a study of the first scene of one of Shakespeare's earliest history plays, *1 Henry VI*. This chapter will end the book by analysing the functioning of one particular scenic effect throughout the whole of Shakespeare's last history play, *Henry VIII*.[1] The opening stage direction of the play in Jay Halio's Oxford edition is '*A cloth of state throughout the play*' (1.1.0), which implies that the chair of state, with its canopy, is on stage for every scene.[2] This direction does not appear in the Folio edition of the play, but it is easy to see why some later editors have chosen to supply it. In Act 1, scene 2, for example, the opening stage direction in the Folio text clearly implies the presence of the state, even though it does not mention it explicitly, since it directs the Cardinal to '*[place] himself under the King's feet on his right side*' (1.2.0); and the next stage direction, a few lines later, directs the King to '*[rise] from his state*' (1.2.8).[3] There is thus a sense in which, at least where the King is present and the implied space is a public state room, the throne is taken for granted; and numerous further stage directions, as we shall see, make its presence explicit in a significant number of scenes. We cannot be certain that it would have been on stage throughout the play in early modern productions, but it is worth following through the possibility that it was in order to see how this particular prop functions in the play, how it is used when it is undoubtedly on stage, and what difference its presence would make in those scenes where it is not strictly necessary.

As earlier chapters have shown, the state is a central and essential prop and emblem on the early modern stage, especially in history plays (see Chapters 4 and 5 above in particular); but it is even more dominant in *Henry VIII* than in Shakespeare's earlier plays. Part of the reason for this is that there are no battle scenes in *Henry VIII*; it is entirely focused on the life of the monarch and its impact on the wider state. The fact that the word 'state' could mean both the seat in which the monarch sat and the wider realm over which he ruled is crucial to the world of the play. If the chair of state may be on stage throughout, so too is the word 'state' repeated in the dialogue with notable frequency.[4] The prologue announces that the play contains things that are 'Sad, high, and working, full of state and woe' (3). Halio glosses the first three adjectives as 'solemn, important, and emotionally charged', glossing 'state' here as 'dignity, stateliness'; and certainly a crucial strategy of the play is to present the workings of the state (in the sense of the political unit of the realm) through stateliness, or ceremony. The continuous presence of the throne would be analogous with the play's repeated staging of lengthy processions and other ceremonial events.[5] States work, the play implies, through stateliness. Subjects are obedient to the state because, to some degree, stateliness compels their obedience.

   The first scene demonstrates this in a way that could be read as cynical. The Dukes of Norfolk and Buckingham are discussing the famous meeting between Henry VIII and Francis I of France at the Field of Cloth of Gold. Buckingham is lamenting the fact that sickness prevented him being there when 'Those suns of glory, those two lights of men, | Met in the vale of Ardres' (1.1.6–7). Norfolk, who was there, tells him:

> Then you lost
> The view of earthly glory. Men might say
> Till this time pomp was single, but now married
> To one above itself. Each following day
> Became the next day's master, till the last
> Made former wonders its. (13–18)

Stateliness, in other words, outdid itself. The speech goes on at much greater length, praising the majesty of the ceremonies and the deeds performed as 'Beyond thought's compass' (36). It may seem a genuine report of wondrous spectacle, or it may seem to go just a touch too far, as Buckingham's brief interjection, 'O, you go far!' (38), suggests. If the empty chair of state is on stage its presence can act both ways: on the one hand it is a ceaseless reminder of the offstage King whose splendour Norfolk reports; and on the other it is, when all is done, no more than an empty throne, in some tension with the magnificence of the reported spectacle.

The talk moves to the Cardinal, who can, according to Buckingham, 'with his very bulk, | Take up the rays o'th'beneficial sun, | And keep it from the earth' (55–7), that is, so fully occupy and take over the King that his (the King's) presence is blocked from his subjects. Again, the emptiness of the throne might speak significantly here; and its silent presence may seem to be alluded to when Norfolk warns Buckingham that: 'The state takes notice of the private difference | Betwixt you and the Cardinal' (101–2). At one level he means the political state and those who jointly share its government; but at another he means the King; and the presence of the empty state here functions as a reminder that spies and informants are everywhere, and that there is nothing said or done, especially at court, that will not eventually get back to the ear of the King. He is a continuous absent presence; and that absent presence becomes more pressing and evident as the scene continues. First, as the detailed stage direction confirms, a display of stateliness enters in formal procession, in the person of Cardinal Wolsey:

Enter Cardinal Wolsey, the purse borne before him, certain of the guard, and two secretaries with papers: The Cardinal in his passage, fixeth his eye on Buckingham, and Buckingham on him, both full of disdain. (114)

In his brief passage over the stage, Wolsey enquires about the Duke of Buckingham's Surveyor (overseer of his estates), and it is evident that he is planning to use the Surveyor to bring Buckingham down. Not only does Wolsey have his informers, but he himself is the King's most elevated informant, as Buckingham knows: 'He's gone to th'King' (128). The sinister underbelly of Wolsey's stately procession becomes nakedly open for a moment. The controlling state uses undercover agency as well as shows of pomp to keep its subjects in order.

As Buckingham rages helplessly against Wolsey, Norfolk tries to warn him against saying too much (the absent throne still reminding the audience, especially after Wolsey's passage, of the King's all-seeing control through Wolsey and his minions). And 'pomp', the word used earlier with seeming approval of the two kings at the Field of Cloth of Gold, takes on a negative aspect as Buckingham applies it to Wolsey, accusing him of planning that same momentous event 'Only to show his pomp as well in France | As here at home' (163–4). The pomp that Wolsey sought to display, Buckingham claims, was his own, not the King's. Buckingham speaks at as great a length as Norfolk did in describing the event with awe first time round; but no sooner has he finished speaking than a Serjeant-at-arms accompanied by guards enters to arrest him for high treason. He is, of course, arrested 'in the name | Of our most sovereign King' (202); and the concept of the King's 'pleasure' is reiterated over the following lines. Lord Abergavenny, Buckingham's son-in-law, arrested moments after Buckingham, responds to the King's pleasure as to the will of God:

> The will of heaven be done and the King's pleasure
> By me obeyed. (215–16)

If the empty state is on stage, Buckingham may look towards it with his closing words:

> I am the shadow of poor Buckingham,
> Whose figure even this instant cloud puts on
> By dark'ning my clear sun. My lords, farewell. (225–7)

The metaphor recalls both the conceit of the kings as suns used by Norfolk in reporting the Field of Cloth of Gold and Buckingham's own earlier reference to Wolsey as coming between the sun and the earth 'with his very bulk'.

The state is certainly on stage in Act 1, scene 2, though it is the stage direction at line 8 rather than the opening stage direction which makes that clear (again perhaps implying that its presence is taken for granted). The opening stage direction is primarily concerned with signalling the relationship between the King and the Cardinal: '*Enter King Henry, leaning on the Cardinal's shoulder...the Cardinal places himself under the King's feet on his right side.*' The King's leaning on Wolsey's shoulder of course signals his increasing dependency on the Cardinal, and Wolsey's placing of himself at the King's feet on his right demonstrates the confidence with which he occupies the position of greatest honour below the King. (The term '*under the King's feet'* alludes to the fact that the King sits on the state, which in turn is on a raised dais. Wolsey sits below the dais.) Spatial position encodes the important facts about the rule of the kingdom: the King sits at the apex of the state, raised and central; but Wolsey, his Lord Chancellor, holder of the Great Seal, is both literally and metaphorically his right-hand man, indispensable to the rule of the kingdom.

The dialogue opens with the King's thanks to Wolsey for protecting him from Buckingham's treachery, a potentially ironic moment following Buckingham's closing words at the end of Act 1, scene 1, indicating that Wolsey must have bribed Buckingham's Surveyor to provide supposed evidence of Buckingham's treason. But talk of Buckingham is immediately interrupted by the entry of the Queen, who kneels before the King. Again, the spatial code, or here its disruption, speaks powerfully. The Queen's rightful place is on the dais, seated next to the King, on his left; and the King signals this by seeking to raise her from her kneeling position: '*King riseth from his state, takes her up, kisses and placeth her by him*' (9). Though she emphasizes the need to kneel on this occasion, because she has something to request from the King, he is equally emphatic that she belongs beside him, not below him:

> Arise, and take place by us...
> you have half our power,
> The other moiety ere you ask is given.
> Repeat your will and take it. (11–14)

Yet the truth is that the King and Queen do not share power half and half. The real co-holder of power in the kingdom is Wolsey, who is proceeding in ways the King is unaware of; and this is Katherine's point. She comes to petition the King to relieve the commons of the excessive taxes imposed on them by Wolsey; and the King's reply tells the audience what they need to know about relative power: 'Taxation? | Wherein? And what taxation?' (38–9). He is completely unaware of Wolsey's actions.

Wolsey's defence incorporates a striking use of the state as metaphor. Taking action, he says, is a crucial requirement for a true statesman; and those who take action must expect others to interpret it wrongly or fail to see what is truly best and worst in such actions.

'If we stand still' and do nothing, fearing the criticism that might follow action, he says:

> We should take root here where we sit
> Or sit state-statues only. (88–9)

Halio, following A. R. Humphreys, glosses this line as 'effigies of statesmen'; but the force of 'state' meaning 'throne' is potentially equally strong in this metaphor. Given that the King is, at the very moment Wolsey speaks, sitting still in his chair of state, the idea of the 'state-statue' could refer primarily to a ruler who sits still in his state, rather than moving out of it to take action. By implication, it could refer to Henry himself, who takes his seat as King, but leaves Wolsey to take control of actually running the kingdom. That control is nowhere more clearly seen than in the part Wolsey plays in questioning Buckingham's Surveyor over the remainder of this scene. Though Wolsey says much less than Henry, he knows when to interject and what to say to make sure that Buckingham will be condemned.

Henry is absent in person from the next scene, where the Lord Chamberlain and Lord Sands discuss the new fashions at court, a new proclamation, and Wolsey's forthcoming banquet. The talk is careful, seeming to praise Wolsey's generosity, whilst perhaps hinting that it is indicative of a stature and wealth beyond measure. The presence of the empty throne in this scene might be felt, as so often in this play, as indicative of the feeling amongst Henry's courtiers that they are always under surveillance. Following on Buckingham's condemnation for treason on the basis of mere report, the implications of speaking too openly or making an enemy by giving offence are all too clear.

The state appears in the opening stage direction for Act 1, scene 4, but this time, significantly, it serves as Wolsey's seat: '*Hautboys. A small table under a state for the Cardinal, a longer table for the guests.*' In fictional terms, of course, this is a wholly different seat—Wolsey's own seat in his own residence—but in real terms it is the same seat that has been on stage from the beginning, the same seat that the King alone has occupied up to now. Its translation into Wolsey's seat here, following the resentment expressed by Buckingham and others at the elevation of this 'butcher's cur' (1.1.120) to such closeness to the King, functions to confirm the naked ambition and inflated self-regard of which others accuse him. The audience sees him literally sitting in the King's seat, under the King's cloth of state. In sitting alone at a separate table from the rest of the company, furthermore, he is also aping regal practice. It was the King's prerogative to dine alone.[6] Though the King appears disguised amongst other maskers in this scene, thus creating the occasion for Wolsey to hint gracefully at the presence of 'one amongst 'em by his person | More worthy this place than myself' (81–2), the courteous pleasantry of the exchange does not fully neutralize the sense the scene creates that Wolsey is the real power behind the throne. His occupation of that very throne speaks at least as potently as the elaborate game of mistaken identity.

The following scene, 2.1, represents a kind of scene characteristic of this play: two or more figures reporting and commenting on the great events of the day. Here the crucial event at the scene's centre is Buckingham's trial, and the presence of the empty state reminds the audience of the King's control over the lives of all those at court, from the highest and most respected (Buckingham) to the lowest and most anonymous (the unnamed Gentlemen who speak together here). This scene shows the operations of the state at their most harsh and unrelenting. It opens at a point where Buckingham's trial has found him guilty and 'All's now done but the ceremony | Of bringing back the prisoner' (4–5). The state has unleashed the full force of its legal and ceremonial machinery on Buckingham and pronounced the death sentence on him. Throughout the First Gentleman's account of the trial, the empty state on stage speaks of the all-powerful political state; and its presence becomes even more intensely focused and malignant when the ceremony of bringing back the prisoner is performed on stage: '*Enter Buckingham from his arraignment, tipstaves before him the axe with the edge towards him, halberds on each side…*'(54). He addresses the common people (and of course speaks directly to the audience in so doing), proclaiming his innocence but at the same time excusing the state as just and forgiving those who sought his death. As he prepares to board the barge that will take him to the Tower, Sir Nicholas Vaux orders an attendant to

> See the barge be ready,
> And fit it with such furniture as suits
> The greatness of his person; (99–101)

but Buckingham's reply is deeply poignant:

> Nay, Sir Nicholas,
> Let it alone; my state now will but mock me. (101–2)

This rejection of all further ceremony, together with his choice of words here, pointedly implies a questioning (less Buckingham's than the play's) of the empty shows of state. The emptiness of the chair of state on stage becomes momentarily emblematic at this point, a reminder that the great spectacles of state are no more than that: mere shows manufactured to give seeming dignity to the machiavellian manoeuvres that underpin the state in fact. As Sir Henry Wotton, a contemporary spectator of *Henry VIII*, commented, the play was 'set forth with many extraordinary circumstances of Pomp and Majesty... sufficient in truth within a while to make greatness very familiar, if not ridiculous'.[7]

Yet the scene makes the point very clearly that a single word from the King may change, or indeed end, a life. Buckingham's father was beheaded without trial by Richard III; Henry VII restored the dukedom to his son, the present Duke of Buckingham; but now the pendulum has swung back with Henry VII's son:

> Now his son,
> Henry the Eighth, life, honour, name, and all
> That made me happy, at one stroke has taken
> For ever from the world. (116–19)

The scene ends with a return to the conversation of the two Gentlemen, which cuts off abruptly with the recognition that they are 'too open here to argue this' (168). The empty state only seems empty; it is watching them as it watched Buckingham and has the same power over their lives.

Act 2, scene 2 shows another, more nobly born, group in discussion. Again the empty state 'hears' as they discuss the King's plans to end his marriage with Queen Katherine and the efforts of Wolsey, the 'King-Cardinal' (18), to help him. He, even more than the King, has their lives in his hands. As the Duke of Norfolk says:

> All men's honours
> Lie like one lump before him to be fashioned
> Into what pitch he please. (47–9)

The whole scene shows how much anxiety and effort all those at court expend on trying to assess the mood and intention of both the King and the Cardinal. Sixty lines into the scene the King is discovered *'reading pensively'* in his closet (that is, in the discovery space at the rear of the stage).[8] There are thus at this point two images of the King juxtaposed: the empty state and the King himself, in private meditation. Suffolk and Norfolk nervously discuss his mood, and soon find themselves the object of Henry's anger:

> SUFFOLK How sad he looks! Sure he is much afflicted.
> KING HENRY Who's there? Ha?
> NORFOLK   Pray God he be not angry.
> KING HENRY Who's there, I say? How dare you thrust yourselves
>   Into my private meditations! (62–5)

Though the King's surveillance of his subjects may be taken for granted, as the presence of the empty state would imply, any intrusion into or observation of his own privacy represents an outrageous breach of protocol.

The following scene shows a conversation between Anne Boleyn and an Old Lady, and their subject is the same subject that is making Henry tense: his divorce. As Anne denies any interest in being a queen, the presence of the empty state becomes deeply ironic, since Henry knows a good deal more than Anne is prepared to admit here. Were Anne not willing and eager to become his wife, he would have no reason to divorce Katherine. This is equally clear to the Old Lady, who openly accuses Anne of hypocrisy and points up her knowledge of Anne's intention to have the King with several obscene double entendres. When the Lord Chamberlain arrives bearing news of the King's decision to honour Anne with the title of Marchioness of Pembroke, it is as though the empty state speaks to clarify Anne's status.

As Anne and the Old Lady exit, with Anne warning the Old Lady not to speak of this to Queen Katherine, the scene cuts immediately to Katherine's trial. Here a very elaborate opening stage direction first scripts a processional entry, then moves to describe the layout of the court in a way that makes clear the central importance of the King seated in his state:

The King takes place under the cloth of state. The two Cardinals sit under him as judges. The Queen takes place some distance from the King. The Bishops place themselves on each side the court in manner of a consistory: Below them the scribes. The lords sit next the Bishops. The rest of the attendants stand in convenient order about the stage. (2.4.0)

The idea of rightful place is key to this direction. The processional entry first orders the trial participants in hierarchical sequence, and the seating then confirms the social order with the King at the apex, the Cardinals below him, and, for the purposes of this trial, the Queen at some distance from the King rather than seated on his left. Bishops, Lords, and Scribes are also in their rightful places, and even the Attendants are to stand 'in convenient [appropriate] order'. All is to be scrupulously correct and subject to the authority of the state in the shape of the King, who is, ahistorically, set above rather than below the Cardinals, appointed as judges of the trial.[9]

Henry is thus made the supreme authority in this scene, whereas in fact he was subject to the jurisdiction of the Cardinals on this occasion. But the scene shows him overruling the judges from the very start:

> CARDINAL WOLSEY Whilst our commission from Rome is read
> Let silence be commanded.
> KING HENRY   What's the need?
> It hath already publicly been read,
> And on all sides th'authority allowed.
> You may then spare that time.
> CARDINAL WOLSEY   Be't so. Proceed. (2.4.1–5)

The scene proceeds with the summons to King Henry and Queen Katherine. Henry, comfortably enthroned in his state, answers 'Here'; but the stage direction makes much of the distance between Henry and his Queen when she is summoned:

The Queen makes no answer, rises out of her chair, goes about the court, comes to the King, and kneels at his feet. (10)

The physical distance between them measures the emotional distance they have travelled since Act 1, scene 2, when Katherine's kneeling moved Henry to stand up out of his state in order to raise her up, kiss her, and place her by him. Now he sits in state while she speaks at length of the injustice done to her; and her former humility gives way to a new defiance: a refusal to accept Wolsey as her judge or to be ruled by the authority of the court. Stage directions meticulously specify that she curtsies to the King as she offers to depart (119), but this appearance of obedience is neutralized by her refusal to return when she is called back to the court. As she says to the anxious Griffith, urging the command to return upon her:

> They vex me past my patience. Pray you, pass on.
> I will not tarry; no, nor ever more
> Upon this business my appearance make
> In any of their courts. (127–30)

Even here, then, where the chair of state is occupied and the state seeks to insist upon its control over even the Queen, Katherine proves that it is possible to resist that insistence. She defies both King and court in leaving, and even the King is overcome, prompted to a paean of praise by her 'true nobility' here and throughout their marriage. The trial proceeds, but can reach no conclusion without the Queen; and it is with bad-tempered abruptness against the Cardinals that Henry orders the court broken up at the end of the scene.

The next scene shifts to show Katherine in a domestic environment, with her women, '*as at work*' (3.1.0). The presence of the empty state in this scene would cast a deep shadow of blame over Henry as Katherine seeks to dispel her troubles with music at the start of the scene. But the King's presence is soon more materially present than in the empty state, when the Cardinals arrive, sent by Henry to try to persuade Katherine to retire quietly to a nunnery rather than continue to oppose the King. Her defiance remains strong and she refuses; but the King's absent presence obtrudes itself again in her closing speech, when she bids the Cardinals:

> Pray do my service to his majesty.
> He has my heart yet, and shall have my prayers
> While I shall have my life. (178–80)

Like all others in the play, but more so, her life is shaped by the King; but her love and loyalty remain pointedly unqualified by her treatment at his hands.

Act 3, scene 2, like Act 2, scene 2, shows Norfolk, Suffolk, and others again discussing the King and Wolsey and trying to read the intentions of both. The emptiness of the state might stand as emblematic in these scenes both of the King's ever-present promi-nence in their thoughts and of his opaqueness to them. They know that he has found '[m]atter against' Wolsey (20); that he has secretly married Anne Boleyn; and that a new favourite, Thomas Cranmer, is about to become Archbishop of Canterbury. Yet there is always more that they do not know. Every new frown or smile must be carefully observed and interpreted. We see Norfolk following every nuance of Wolsey's mood when he enters:

> NORFOLK   Observe, observe; he's moody.
>   . . .
> He's discontented.
>   . . .
>   He is vexed at something; (75–105)

and the close sequence of observation is immediately reminiscent of the anxious observation of the King in the earlier scene (2.2).[10] Here the empty throne may seem to suggest a fluidity of occupancy: does the King rule Wolsey or Wolsey rule the King?

Yet, as Wolsey himself knows, 'An heretic, an arch-one, Cranmer, one | Hath crawled into the favour of the King | And is his oracle' (103–5). There is a third contender for the power of the state; and immediately following these lines the King himself enters, '*reading a schedule*', and Wolsey's fall begins. At the end of this scene, after Henry has left, Wolsey undergoes the same experience as Bucking-ham did in Act 1. The King's death-blow is delivered to him by others bearing the fateful message:

> NORFOLK Hear the King's pleasure, Cardinal, who commands you
>   To render up the Great Seal presently
>   Into our hands. (229–31)

Wolsey tries to insist on the King's own presence in person:

> CARDINAL WOLSEY   Now, who'll take it?
> SURREY The King that gave it.
> CARDINAL WOLSEY   It must be himself then; (251–2)

but his opposition unleashes a torrent of insults from the noblemen sent to deliver the King's command. Wolsey and Cromwell remain on stage after the others leave, weeping for this outcome. Wolsey may turn towards the empty state as he delivers the closing lines of the scene: 'Farewell | The hopes of court; my hopes in heaven do dwell' (459–60).

The two Gentlemen through whose eyes we saw Buckingham's trial reappear in Act 4, scene 1 for the coronation procession of Queen Anne, so that it is seen through their eyes. The presence of an empty state in this scene would re-emphasize the fact that in this play the watchers are always also watched, and the King's choices determine and limit the choices of all his subjects. Again they break off as their conversation moves into dangerous territory—talk of falling stars, which refers to both politics and sex. Wolsey falls from the King's grace as Katherine falls from his bed and Anne falls (or rather rises) into it. A third Gentleman recounts the ceremony of coronation itself and the rise of Thomas Cromwell. As always, the events of the play are entirely framed and determined by the King's business. With every one of his smiles or frowns a new star rises or an old one falls (and the play is notably full of references to his frowning).[11] And as always, ceremony enacts the business of the state in such a way as to seek to make it palatable to the people. The substitution of one queen for another and the elevation of Henry's preference over the nation's good is enacted through the overwhelming of ordinary conversation by vast pomp and prolonged spectacle. Much is made of Anne's own sitting in 'a rich chair of state' at her coronation, and of the fact that she departs from the abbey 'with the same full state' (69, 95) as she entered the city. The pointed repetition of the word rhymes with the continuing onstage presence of the key prop.

Katherine, however, the focus of the next scene, is as far from this state-endorsed enthronement as can be. Her entry is the antithesis of Anne's proud procession: '*Enter Katherine Dowager, sick, led between Griffith, her gentleman usher, and Patience her woman*' (4.2.0). Where Anne was erect, Katherine is bent; and where Anne ascended into a throne of state, Katherine has to ask for a chair. The Oxford edition of the play adds '*three chairs*' to the opening stage direction, but this is misleading. A chair was already a sign of some status, and it is unlikely that when Griffith and Patience sit down, later in the scene, they sit on chairs. More probably they would have sat on stools, to retain the distinction between Katherine's status and their own. Sick-chairs, in any case, have a recognizable status of their own on stage, as we have seen (see Chapters 5 and 8 above), and the visual rhyme between the chair of state and the sick-chair which is so visible in the *Henry VI* plays, is also evident here. Katherine's chair rhymes ironically with the empty chair of state; and her sickness points to the diseased authority at the head of this state. The rudeness of the Messenger who comes to her in this scene and fails to kneel highlights the degree to which her present state is distant from her rightful place, made so much of in Act 1, scene 2. The image of the 'unqueened' Katherine (4.2.172), dying in her sick-chair, implicitly condemns the absent King, whose empty state is the only company he brings her in the last moments of her life, despite her undying love for him: 'Tell him, in death I blessed him, | For so I will' (164–5).

Act 5 is dominated by the birth of Elizabeth and the near-fall of Cranmer. Again, all are watching the King at this tense time, as he waits for the birth of the son he so strongly desires, and his frown strikes terror into Cranmer (5.1.88–9). Cranmer, however, unlike most of the men in positions of authority in this play, seems not to know 'how [his] state stands i'th'world' (5.1.128) and to be oblivious to the plotting of others against him. Where up to now the King's chair of state has been the single and dominant image of authority, Henry now produces a ring to give to Cranmer as a further token of his absent presence, should it be needed in time of trouble. As Cranmer leaves, the Old Lady enters with news of the child, and the absurdity of Henry's determination to control everything around him is made almost comic:

> KING HENRY Is the Queen delivered?
>   Say, 'Ay, and of a boy.'
> OLD LADY   Ay, ay, my liege,
>   And of a lovely boy. (5.1.163–5)

Subjects will say what the King wants to hear, however far that may be from the truth. Yet what subjects will say cannot make it so, and the Old Lady has to renege: ''Tis a girl | Promises boys hereafter' (166–7).

The next scene shows Cranmer being kept waiting at the door with 'boys, grooms, and lackeys' (5.2.17) by the King's Council; and more than ever the presence of the empty state in this scene acts as a reminder that the King is keeping watch over the doings of his councillors. This is made even more explicit within a few lines. First Dr Butts, the King's Physician, sees their behaviour and reports it to the King; and following that information, the King himself appears with Dr Butts '*at a window above*' (18). The surveillance is now explicit and doubly emphatic: the empty state sits centrally on the stage, as throughout, and the King in person surveys the scene from above. The King then instructs Butts to draw the curtain, allowing them to hear all that will pass below without being seen. Another full stage direction sets the scene for the Council meeting (implying by its wording the already given and continuous presence of the state):

A council table brought in with chairs and stools, and placed under the state. Enter Lord Chancellor, places himself at the upper end of the table, on the left hand: a seat being left void above him, as for Canterbury's seat. (34)

As the subsequent action makes clear, Henry's state, already on stage, is different from the '*seat*' that is left '*void*' for the Archbishop of Canterbury. Cranmer, the Archbishop, is on trial and hence cannot occupy his usual and rightful place; the parallel with Queen Katherine, demoted from her rightful place to become a mere subject on trial, is self-evident.

As Cranmer is brought in, the Lord Chancellor's opening words point up Cranmer's empty seat with regret:

> My good lord Archbishop, I'm very sorry
> To sit here at this present and behold
> That chair stand empty. (42–4)

The Council proceeds to charge him with heresy and, as others have done before in arresting Buckingham and Wolsey, invokes 'his highness' pleasure' (86) as the motivating force behind its decision to commit Cranmer to the Tower. As Cranmer is about to be taken away under guard he produces the King's ring, thereby invoking a very different concept of the King's pleasure. At last the seemingly unstoppable mechanism of falling from the King's favour is to take a different turn. Now that the ring has stopped the flow of events, the King must enter to occupy his state and take control on stage: '*Enter King frowning on them, takes his seat*' (147). Emphasis shifts from the omniscient surveillance of the empty throne to the actual presence of the King, who dismisses Gardiner's unctuous welcome as flattery 'too thin and base to hide offences' in his very presence (159). And, as in Act 1, scene 2, when Henry's concern was to seat his Queen in her rightful place, he now reinstates Cranmer at the head of the Council table with strong threats against any who may dare to question his place:

> By all that's holy, he had better starve
> Than but once think this place becomes thee not. (166–7)

The play moves towards its climax, the christening of Princess Elizabeth, with another scene in the now-familiar mode of showing ceremony or the preparations for it through the eyes of more marginal figures, such as the Gentlemen. Here, in Act 5, scene 3, the Porter and his Man are seen trying to hold back the crowd pressing to see the christening. They are the instruments of the empty state on stage, seeking to police the space of the court by trying to keep out those uninvited guests who are forcing their way in. When the Lord Chamberlain comes in and finds them failing to exclude their 'faithful friends o'th'suburbs' (69), his immediate reaction is to tell them that if the King's anger falls on him he will transfer the impact to them by fining them for neglect. The sense that the King's frowns determine the lives of all beneath him in the commonwealth never leaves the play.

The final scene (5.4) brings the entire court on stage again in a full ceremonial entry, outlined in the usual detail in the opening stage direction, with a separate entry for King Henry, escorted by the guard. There is no stage direction indicating whether Henry stands or takes his seat in the chair of state, but if the seat has been on stage throughout the play its presence would really require that the King take his seat in it to give the play a sense of closure. The length of Cranmer's speech prophesying wonders for this future queen would also conduce to a seated position for the King, though most of the court would probably remain standing. The image of the King seated in his state, at the centre of a full stage celebrating the birth of a new heir, encourages the audience towards a feeling of resolution and completeness, a feeling that everything and everyone is in their rightful place and all is well with the English state. The play, however, is much more complex and ambivalent than such a conclusion might suggest; and the continuous visibility of the chair of state, this chapter has argued, has as much potential for creating images of mixed or negative resonance as for creating this positive concluding stage picture.

What contemporary audiences would have made of the mixed tones in the play is difficult to recover at this distance in time. Henry Wotton is the only contemporary spectator on record and he was not impressed. Famously, of course, he saw only the first act of the play, since a cannon shot in Act 1, scene 4 set fire to the thatch and burnt the Globe down. But for those who saw it right through, before and in the immediate aftermath of the Globe fire, the play, first performed ten years after the accession of James I, must have created some pointed areas of comparison between the present monarch and his predecessors, Henry VIII and Elizabeth I. Whether or not the chair of state was on stage throughout the performance, its recurrent and potent presence repeatedly directs the spectators' focus back to the power of the monarch and the state and invites them to ask some hard questions about the way they function in the life of the nation.

Notes

INTRODUCTION

1. *1 Henry VI*, 1.1.0. (Future references will be in brackets in the text.)
2. The presence of a funeral carriage is implied in Exeter's comparison of himself and his fellow-mourners to 'captives bound to a triumphant car' (line 22); and the wearing of mourning robes is indicated in Bedford's reference to 'these disgraceful wailing robes' (line 86). More detail on mourning robes, which differed according to the status of the wearer, can be found in Jennifer Woodward, *The Theatre of Death: The Ritual Management of Royal Funerals in Renaissance England, 1570–1625* (Woodbridge: Boydell Press, 1997), 19–21.
3. The so-called 'Diary' of Philip Henslowe, owner of the Rose theatre, shows that the Admiral's Men regularly bought clothes from pawnbrokers and other clothing dealers, and there is also evidence that the Revels Office sometimes gave the costumes worn for court performances to the players in payment. See further Jean McIntyre and Garrett P. J. Epp, '"Cloathes worth all the rest": Costumes and Properties', in John D. Cox and David Scott Kastan (eds.), *A New History of Early English Drama* (New York: Columbia University Press, 1997), 279 and n. 2.
4. Quoted in Andrew Gurr, *The Shakespearean Stage, 1574–1642*, 3rd edn. (Cambridge: Cambridge University Press, 1992), 194.
5. Illustrations of the funeral of Elizabeth I in British Library MS Add. 35324 are available through Images Online at the British Library. See especially the illustration on fo. 37ᵛ, image 057867, reproduced at http://www.imagesonline.bl.uk/results.asp?image=057867&imagex=3&searchnum=2. A further manuscript, BL Add. 5408, also has drawings of Elizabeth's funeral procession. The Reformation did of course bring some changes to funeral ritual, but there was a good deal of continuity between early Tudor and post-Reformation funerals (see Woodward, *Theatre of Death*, chapter 2).
6. *1 Henry VI*, ed. Taylor, 15.
7. *Henslowe's Diary*, ed. R. A. Foakes, 2nd edn. (Cambridge: Cambridge University Press, 2002), 16–20; *1 Henry VI*, ed. Taylor, 2.

8. Good brief summaries of what is known about each of the early play-houses are to be found in Glynne Wickham, Herbert Berry, and William Ingram (eds.), *English Professional Theatre, 1530–1660* (Cambridge: Cambridge University Press, 2000). Scholarship on these playhouses continues to be updated, however, so numerous later publications contain revised information about the playhouses, especially those that it has been possible to excavate: the Rose and the Globe. See e.g. Julian Bowsher and Pat Miller, *The Rose and the Globe: Playhouses of Shakespeare's Bankside, Southwark: Excavations 1988–91* (London: Museum of London Archaeology, 2009).

9. Most of Shakespeare's histories were written before 1599. The only two plays that could have been first performed at the Globe were *Henry V* and *Henry VIII*. The latter play literally set the Globe on fire in 1613 and thus became the cause of its rebuilding in 1614.

10. Although the Globe was built using the timber salvaged from the Theatre, it is unlikely that it was built to precisely the same dimensions and plan as the Theatre. The legal documents relating to the dismantling of the Theatre indicate that the timber was set up on the new premises 'in another form'. See Bowsher and Miller, *The Rose and the Globe*, 90. For evidence that both actors and spectators used the gallery see Richard Hosley, 'The Gallery over the Stage in the Public Playhouse of Shakespeare's Time', *Shakespeare Quarterly*, 8 (1957), 15–31.

11. Two very useful introductions to early theatre design are Gurr, *Shakespearean Stage*, and Andrew Gurr and Mariko Ichikawa, *Staging in Shakespeare's Theatres* (Oxford: Oxford University Press, 2000).

12. Most books on early theatre history reproduce the De Witt drawing, which is also easily found on the internet. See e.g. Gurr, *Shakespearean Stage*, 133.

13. Irving Wardle, *Independent on Sunday*, 14 August 1994, cited in Randall Martin's introduction to *3 Henry VI*, 77.

14. 'Stagecraft and Imagery in Shakespeare's *Henry VI*', *Yearbook of English Studies*, 23 (1993), 66.

15. The sequence in which the First Tetralogy (composed of the three parts of *Henry VI* and *Richard III*) was written remains controversial. (The term 'First Tetralogy', furthermore, is sometimes used to imply the view that the four plays were planned as a sequence; but here I use the terms 'First Tetralogy' and 'Second Tetralogy' without that implication, merely to distinguish the two groups of four into which these eight plays fall.) Some critics believe that Part One of *Henry VI* was the first to be written, whilst others believe that Part Two pre-dated it. The question is further complicated by the fact that Parts Two and Three are related to two plays that some

believe to be corrupt versions of these same plays and others take to be plays by other dramatists that became sources for Shakespeare. (These plays were respectively entitled *The First Part of the Contention betwixt the Two Famous Houses of York and Lancaster*, printed in 1594, and *The True Tragedy of Richard Duke of York*, printed in 1595.) Furthermore, as noted above, the scene may be the work of Thomas Nashe or another collaborator, with or without Shakespeare. (David Bevington summarizes the debate on these matters in his essay on *1 Henry VI* in Richard Dutton and Jean E. Howard (eds.), *A Companion to Shakespeare's Works*, ii: *The Histories* (Oxford: Blackwell, 2003), 308–11.) The term 'first' in the First Tetralogy, however, refers to the fact that it was written first. The so-called Second Tetralogy (consisting of *Richard II*, the two parts of *Henry IV*, and *Henry V*) deals with a period of history earlier than the first; while *King John* and *Henry VIII*, which stand outside of any series of plays, deal respectively with periods well before and somewhat later than the two tetralogies. *Edward III*, which may be partly by Shakespeare, but is not covered in this book, deals with the period immediately preceding the Second Tetralogy.

16. Shakespeare dramatizes Agincourt as though it were the final event in the conquest of France; but in fact years of further conflict followed Agincourt (1415). Henry did not marry Catherine de Valois, daughter of Charles VI of France, until 1420, and he continued his campaign in France until his death in 1422. The Hundred Years War is continuing as *1 Henry VI* opens, and continued until 1453, a point represented in the play by the battle in which the Talbots die at 4.7.

17. On rehearsal practices see further Tiffany Stern, *Making Shakespeare: From Stage to Page* (London: Routledge, 2004); and on spatial codes in the early modern period see further Janette Dillon, *The Language of Space in Court Performance, 1400–1625* (Cambridge: Cambridge University Press, 2010).

18. John of Gaunt, grandfather of Henry V, sired two lines of descendants. Henry IV, father of Henry V and the brothers who mourn him in this scene, was the son of his first wife, Blanche; whilst the Beauforts were born out of wedlock to his mistress Katherine Swynford, and legitimized only when she later became John of Gaunt's wife. Clear genealogical tables and fuller accounts of the historical background to all Shakespeare's English history plays may be consulted in Peter Saccio, *Shakespeare's English Kings: History, Chronicle, and Drama* (Oxford: Oxford University Press, 1977).

19. 'Pageants into Play: Shakespeare's Three Perspectives on Idea and Image', in David M. Bergeron (ed.), *Pageantry in the Shakespearean Theater* (Athens, Ga.: University of Georgia Press, 1985), 227.

20. As Taylor's note to this passage points out, Shakespeare is here telescoping twenty-five years of history and distorting the facts for dramatic impact. Orléans and Poitiers could not be lost because they were never won in the first place.

21. Brecht, who drew on Shakespearian theatre for many of his ideas, may have derived the notion of the *Gestus* (combining both gist and gesture) from this kind of performance; and, as Brecht's translator, John Willett, points out, the obsolete English term 'gest', together with its adjective, is useful in translating Brecht's *Gestus*, for which there are no precise modern English equivalents (*Brecht on Theatre*, ed. and trans. John Willett (London: Methuen, 1964), 42). In the absence of such equivalents, these terms can thus be useful too in writing about Shakespeare's dramaturgy, and they will crop up occasionally in this book. Editors of the play disagree as to whether Bedford literally removes his cloak as he speaks of doing so (see Taylor's note to these lines on p. 102).

22. A stage direction in Middleton's *A Chaste Maid in Cheapside* specifying entry '*at one door*' and '*At the other door*' confirms the two doors at the Swan, but a stage direction in *Eastward Ho*, for example, indicates the presence of three doors at the Blackfriars Theatre. Most scholars believe that the Globe had three doors, but no stage direction or other evidence confirms this; and the number of doors at the Theatre and the Curtain is not known. See further the entry on 'door' in Alan C. Dessen and Leslie Thomson, *A Dictionary of Stage Directions in English Drama, 1580–1642* (Cambridge: Cambridge University Press, 1999), 73–4.

23. See e.g. David Bradley, *From Text to Performance in the Elizabethan Theatre: Preparing the Play for the Stage* (Cambridge: Cambridge University Press, 1992) and Tim Fitzpatrick and Daniel Johnston, 'Spaces, Doors and Places in Early Modern English Staging', *Theatre Notebook*, 63 (2009), 2–19.

24. See, for example, the analysis of Acts 3–5 of *The Tempest* in Mick Wallis and Simon Shepherd, *Studying Plays*, 2nd edn. (London: Arnold, 2002), 98–102. This form of analysis is known as French scene analysis.

CHAPTER 2

1. G. K. Hunter coined the useful phrase 'energizing [a] locale' for scenes where location is important ('Flatcaps and Bluecoats: Visual Signals on the Elizabethan Stage', *Essays and Studies* (1980), 23). Hamlet, he says, 'is not energizing any locale' when he utters his first soliloquy. Jack Cade and Alexander Iden below, by contrast, are strongly energizing the locale of the garden.

2. In *The First Part of the Contention* (see Chapter 1 n. 15 above) the two enter simultaneously, Cade '*at one door*' and Iden '*at the other*' (see the edition prepared by William Montgomery (Oxford: Malone Society, 1985), line 1927).

3. Cade's speech plays on the two meanings of 'sallet': a herb or salad leaf and a type of helmet.

4. Raphael Holinshed, *Chronicles of England, Scotland and Ireland*, [ed. Henry Ellis], 6 vols. (London: J. Johnson etc., 1807), iii. 227 (Holinshed's source is Stow at this point). The 'Iden' spelling originates with the chronicler Edward Hall (see Geoffrey Bullough, *Narrative and Dramatic Sources of Shakespeare*, 8 vols. (London: Routledge and Kegan Paul, 1957–75), iii. 118). Holinshed's *Chronicles*, and particularly the revised edition of 1587, completed after his death, was a collaborative work. Holinshed worked with Reyner Wolfe, his printer, on the first edition of 1577, and a team of writers, led by Abraham Fleming and including John Stow, worked on the second edition. Though I will continue to use the name 'Holinshed' as a form of reference here in distinguishing this chronicle from others, this should be understood as shorthand in relation to the multi-authored 1587 edition. Holinshed and his co-authors, like other early modern historians, frequently followed their sources word for word. This is one reason why it can sometimes be difficult to tell whether Shakespeare was following Hall or Holinshed, since he evidently knew both sources well.

5. It is always difficult to estimate, of course, what proportion of a popular audience would understand these kinds of references. See further Dillon, *Language of Space*, 14–15 and 21.

6. 'Villain' was primarily a social, not a moral, term, meaning 'serf' (the lowest position in a feudal society), and a shearman was a clothworker.

7. 'Pageants into Play', 221. Bertolt Brecht's didactic dramaturgy was of course partly based on his knowledge of Shakespeare, but, while Brecht understood the value of parables for making his audience think, he did not generally combine realism and pageantry in quite the way Shakespeare and his contemporaries did.

8. Peter Roberts, reviewing the RSC production of 1963, quoted in *2 Henry VI*, ed. Roger Warren, 55.

9. *Shakespearean Design* (Cambridge, Mass.: Belknap Press, 1972), 9.

10. Severed heads also constitute speaking pictures. See further Chapter 5 below.

11. Holinshed is here quoted from appendix E in *Richard III*, ed. John Jowett, 392.

12. Holinshed's preface to the reader offers this justification for incorporating the work of earlier historians without alteration: 'For my part, I have in

things doubtful rather chosen to show the diversity of their writings, than by overruling them, and using a peremptory censure, to frame them to agree to my liking: leaving it nevertheless to each man's judgement, to control them as he seeth cause' (quoted in Warren Chernaik, *The Cambridge Introduction to Shakespeare's History Plays* (Cambridge: Cambridge University Press, 2007), 2).

13. Quoted in Paola Pugliatti, *Shakespeare the Historian* (New York: St Martin's Press, 1996), 33.

14. The conversation with William Lambarde in which Elizabeth famously said 'I am Richard II. Know ye not that?' is reprinted in Peter Ure's Arden edition of *Richard II* (5th edn. (London: Methuen, 1961), lix).

15. Peter Blayney gives a clear account of these processes in 'The Publication of Playbooks', in Cox and Kastan (eds.), *New History of Early English Drama*, especially 396–405. I am here using the word 'license' more loosely than Blayney.

16. Pugliatti, *Shakespeare the Historian*, 6.

17. The word 'chronicle' in Tudor histories, however, was much more loosely used, and both Hall and Holinshed were known primarily as writers of 'chronicles' despite the fact that their works formed a sequence of linear narratives. I will therefore keep the word 'annal' for the narrower use, and use the term 'chronicle' as Tudor writers and readers did, to mean simply written history.

18. Michael Hattaway argues that the Kentish garden 'turns out to be another failed paradise in which ideals are vitiated by ambition', since Iden goes off at the close of the scene 'to claim the honour that he knows will be his reward' (introduction to *The Second Part of King Henry VI* (Cambridge: Cambridge University Press, 1991), 34). It is certainly the case that Iden's Eden is problematized by Cade's death, but the motivation for this act of violence is not ambition but the wish to defend self and property against violent intrusion.

19. These are the terms used in the Folio text's stage directions and/or speech headings. 'Lady' and 'gentleman' are parallel terms implying a certain level of wealth and respectability; but the term 'lady' remains the female parallel of male status up to the level of knight and, used broadly, of landed aristocracy. Thus a countess or a duchess, for example, is also a lady, whereas an earl or a duke would never be described as a mere gentleman. Gentlemen, as Thomas Smith wrote in 1583, were 'made good cheap in England', and anyone who could 'live idly and without manual labour' could be counted a gentleman (*De Republica Anglorum*, cited in John D. Cox, *Shakespeare and the Dramaturgy of Power* (Princeton: Princeton University

Press, 1989), 53). A porter, as a worker in paid employment, is of more lowly status than ladies and gentlemen. Authorship of these scenes is generally attributed as follows: 2.1 (disputed but mostly thought to be by Fletcher); 2.3 (Shakespeare); 4.1 (Fletcher); 5.1 (Shakespeare); and 5.3 (Fletcher).

20. For this and other cynical views about ceremony expressed in Shakespeare's time see Dillon, *Language of Space*, 20–1.
21. *King Henry VIII* (London: Arden, 2000), 98.
22. On the matter of the King's 'conscience', see further *King Henry VIII*, ed. McMullan, 80–5, and Janette Dillon, 'The Trials of Queen Katherine in *Henry VIII*', *Shakespeare Survey*, 63 (2010), 155–6.
23. The lines from Holinshed are cited in McMullan's note to lines 82–92 of this scene.
24. McMullan argues, rightly, I think, that this scene also has a much bigger comment to make on the themes of the play, and that it is 'in many ways paradigmatic of the play as a whole in its resistance to the formalities of Reformation' (*King Henry VIII*, 144–7).
25. *King Henry VIII*, 103.
26. In describing the Alienation Effect he wanted from his actors, for example, Brecht wrote that 'the actor's attitude should be one of a man who is astounded and contradicts'. Nothing should be taken as given, 'as something that "was bound to turn out that way"'...Before memorizing the words he must memorize what he felt astounded at and where he felt impelled to contradict' (*Brecht on Theatre*, ed. Willett, 137).

CHAPTER 3

1. Cf. the Duke of Norfolk's description of Wolsey's behaviour in *Henry VIII*:

> Some strange commotion
> Is in his brain. He bites his lip, and starts,
> Stops on a sudden, looks upon the ground,
> Then lays his finger on his temple; straight
> Springs out into fast gait, then stops again,
> Strikes his breast hard, and anon he casts
> His eye against the moon. In most strange postures
> We have seen him set himself. (3.2.113–20)

2. See further Alan Dessen's studies: *Elizabethan Stage Conventions and Modern Interpreters* (Cambridge: Cambridge University Press, 1984) and *Recovering Shakespeare's Theatrical Vocabulary* (Cambridge: Cambridge University Press, 1995).

3. Joel B. Altman, *The Tudor Play of Mind: Rhetorical Inquiry and the Development of Elizabethan Drama* (Berkeley and Los Angeles: University of California Press, 1978). Mark Rose discusses more fully, with examples, the way Elizabethan training in rhetoric fostered a tendency to think in formal patterns more widely (*Shakespearean Design*, 59–67).

4. *Shakespearean Design*, 10.

5. I discuss issues of space and its meanings much more extensively in my book *The Language of Space*. On spatial protocols especially relevant to the history plays see Chapter 2 on processions and royal entries and Chapter 4 on the reception of ambassadors at court.

6. It is also possible that some of the early history plays may have been written for performance in playhouses that did not have a discovery space.

7. Since a version of this scene occurs in *The True Tragedy of Richard Duke of York*, it may or may not have been Shakespeare's invention. See further Chapter 1 n. 15 above.

8. Evidence for the central position of the molehill on which Henry sits is discussed in Chapter 4 below. Reading this too literally as 'time out' from the battle, however, would be problematic. The time out simply has to happen in the sequence of the play in order to create the space for contemplation.

9. The Oxford editions supplement stage directions with editorial material. The stage direction printed in the First Folio reads: '*Enter a son that hath killed his father, at one door: and a father that hath killed his son at another door*'; and *The True Tragedy of Richard Duke of York* separates it into two directions: '*Enter a soldier with a dead man in his arms*', and '*Enter another soldier with a dead man*' (*The True Tragedy of Richard Duke of York* (London: Thomas Millington, 1595), sig. C2^v, accessed via *Early English Books Online* (*EEBO*) 30 June 2010). The detail that each is carrying a dead body is thus deduced from *The True Tragedy*. See further Randall Martin's note on this stage direction in his edition of the play.

10. The first part of *Henry VI* may of course have been written after the other two parts, but even if it was conceived as a 'prequel', it was with a view to setting the scene for the other two plays.

11. Bullough, *Narrative and Dramatic Sources*, iii. 291.

12. As Emrys Jones points out, the idea for using All Souls, a traditional time for remembrance of the dead, almost certainly came from the historical fact that Buckingham was executed on All Souls' Day 1483. Buckingham's execution actually took place nearly two years before Bosworth (22 August 1485), but dramatically, linking these two events and connecting them to this time of the year, when popular belief held that souls in purgatory might appear to

those who had wronged them in life, would have created a powerful frisson to this scene for early modern audiences (Jones, *The Origins of Shakespeare* (Oxford: Clarendon Press, 1977), 227–9).

13. This technique is sometimes known as 'simultaneous staging'. It was familiar from medieval theatre, where the various scaffolds or 'mansions' designating different places were normally simultaneously on view, though conventionally the audience was used to understanding those inactive at any given point to be absent from the fiction until actors began to play on or around them. Such simultaneous staging is also visible, for example, in *King Lear*, Act 4, scenes 2–4, where Kent is put in the stocks at the end of 2.2 and reappears in them at the opening of 2.4. Edgar, meanwhile, appears in 2.3 in a location understood to be elsewhere; but it is likely that Kent remains visible on stage in the stocks throughout.

14. See e.g. Robert James Fusillo, 'Tents on Bosworth Field', *Shakespeare Quarterly*, 6 (1955), 193–4, and Richard Hosley, 'More About "Tents" on Bosworth Field', *Shakespeare Quarterly*, 7 (1956), 458–9; and see further the entry under 'tent' in Dessen and Thomson, *Dictionary*, 227–8. Property tents certainly appeared on stage in some Elizabethan plays, but, as Dessen and Thomson note, 'the actual presence of property *tents* is . . . hard to determine' (228).

15. It is likely that *Dr Faustus* (probably first written and performed in 1588–9) was written before *Richard III* (1592–3). *The True Tragedy of Richard III* has no equivalent scene. Both *Faustus* and *Richard III* were probably performed at the Theatre. The last documented performance of a mystery cycle was at Coventry in 1579; but cycle drama may have been unfamiliar to London audiences of the sixteenth century. References to religious plays performed at Skinners Well or Clerkenwell, which may have been a form of cycle drama, stop after 1409. For more detail see Anne Lancashire, *London Civic Theatre: City Drama and Pageantry from Roman Times to 1558* (Cambridge: Cambridge University Press, 2002), 54–62.

16. *The End Crowns All: Closure and Contradiction in Shakespeare's History* (Princeton: Princeton University Press, 1991), 91.

17. I here depart from John Jowett's Oxford edition, which takes the Quarto rather than the Folio as its copy text: 'I and I' instead of 'I am I'. Though the Quarto text does, as Jowett points out, emphasize the sense of self-division Richard now experiences following the appearance of the ghosts, the Folio version has affinities with Shakespeare's choice of words both in this play and elsewhere. Cf., for example, Richard's own words at 5.6.83 ('I am myself alone') and the Bastard's claim in *King John* (discussed in Chapter 4 below): 'I am I, howe'er I was begot' (1.1.175).

18. The orations, with the unique stage directions labelling them as such, are curiously separate from the action, despite the fact that they echo its symmetry, and have been thought to be late additions to the text. See further Jowett's appendix D, item 17, 384–5.

19. 'Favours' were objects given as a mark of favour or ceremonial decorations worn as a mark of identity; but here, David Bevington notes in his edition of the play, they are probably 'the twisted silken band in the Prince's colours joining his crest to his helmet...or the plumes of his helmet described in 4.1.98' (*1 Henry IV*, 281).

CHAPTER 4

1. Andrew Gurr reproduces an image of the state used by Queen Elizabeth for the opening of Parliament in 1586 (*Richard II*, ed. Gurr, 2nd edn. (Cambridge: Cambridge University Press: 2003), 40).

2. Shakespeare conflates the first battle of St Albans in 1455 (which ended *2 Henry VI*) with the battle of Northampton in 1460, and begins the play after the latter of the two.

3. Whether Henry himself is angry is not self-evident from his reaction: 'My lords, look where the sturdy rebel sits, | Even in the chair of state' (50–1). Randall Martin, in his Oxford edition, notes the range of ways in which modern actors have interpreted it, from timid chagrin through astonishment to rage.

4. See Jones, *Origins of Shakespeare*, 54, and Martha Hester Fleischer, *The Iconography of the English History Play* (Salzburg: Institut für Englische Sprache und Literatur, Universität Salzburg, 1974), 74–6. John Dover Wilson, in the introduction to his edition of *3 Henry VI*, draws attention to this scene's resemblance to the Passion without specifically mentioning the mystery plays (*The Third Part of King Henry VI* (Cambridge: Cambridge University Press, 1952), xxviii).

5. Bullough, *Narrative and Dramatic Sources*, iii. 210.

6. See David Bevington, *Action is Eloquence: Shakespeare's Language of Gesture* (Cambridge, Mass.: Harvard University Press, 1984), 104.

7. The first pageant for the coronation entry of Elizabeth I, for example, was a three-storeyed structure with Elizabeth at the top and her ancestors, Henry VIII and Anne Boleyn and Henry VII and Elizabeth of York, beneath her.

8. Quoted in Gary Taylor's introduction to *Henry V*, 3.

9. On history plays in the context of war see further David Bevington, *Tudor Drama and Politics* (Cambridge, Mass.: Harvard University Press, 1968), 195–211.

10. See further Bevington, *Action is Eloquence*, 101–3.

11. See *King John*, ed. Braunmuller, Appendix A.2.

12. Alarums and excursions are usually mentioned together in stage directions (as at the opening of 3.2 in *King John*). Technically an excursion is a sortie against the enemy, while an alarum is the sound that accompanies it, a call to arms sounded on the trumpet or other instrument; but in practice 'excursions' made while the armies are offstage (as here in 2.1) must also be sound-effects.

13. Blanche, as Shakespeare's text makes clear, is in fact a 'daughter... of Spain' (424) but is related to the English royal house. She is King John's niece, the offspring of the marriage between John's sister and the King of Castile.

14. Nothing is known about the earliest performances of *King John*, but if it is correctly dated to 1595–6, it was probably first performed at the Theatre, which the Lord Chamberlain's Men were using at that date (and where the number of stage doors is not known for certain). If it remained in repertory up to and beyond 1600 it would probably also have been performed at the Curtain and the Globe.

15. Even more pointedly, and unusually, this rhyming couplet is actually one of two consecutive couplets closing the scene on the same repeated rhyme.

CHAPTER 5

1. *3 Henry VI*, ed. Michael Hattaway (Cambridge: Cambridge University Press, 1993), 14.

2. That combat, however, never takes place, with the result that the panoply of formal preparation for it begins to look like self-parody. Chivalric moments, as suggested in the discussion of Hotspur's death in Chapter 2 above, tend to be presented in a dialogic manner, incorporating their own critique of the chivalric ethos.

3. Dessen, 'Stagecraft and Imagery', 76–8.

4. *Richard III*, ed. Jowett, 80.

5. The book as a prop is ambivalent, and functions differently in different contexts. The prayer book on the pillow of two princes Richard causes to be murdered shortly after this scene is an emblem of their innocent goodness (*Richard III*, 4.3.14). In Henry VI, however, who is regularly seen carrying or reading a book, and is indeed at his book when Richard murders him, the book also signals, besides Henry's piety, a failure to take adequate control as King. His 'bookish rule', according to Richard of York, father of Richard III, 'hath pull'd fair England down' (*2 Henry VI*, 1.1.258). For Jack Cade and the rebels in the same play, the book is a sign

of learning that incites them to fury, and literacy is sufficient reason to hang a man 'with his pen and inkhorn about his neck' (4.2.100–1). On the symbolic functioning of the book as prop see further Bevington, *Action is Eloquence*, 51.

CHAPTER 6

1. 'Prince Hal's Falstaff: Positioning Psychoanalysis and the Female Reproductive Body', in R. J. C. Watt (ed.), *Shakespeare's Early History Plays* (London: Longman, 2002), 113. See also Chapter 7 n. 2 below.

2. *Action is Eloquence*, 49.

3. See further Taylor's note on this character in his edition of the play (*1 Henry VI*, 94).

4. Hall is quoted in Roger Warren's introduction to *2 Henry VI*, 28. Hall also described Joan of Arc as '[t]his witch or manly woman' (Bullough, *Narrative and Dramatic Sources*, iii. 61).

5. The relationship between Margaret and Suffolk in the play is developed from mere hints in the sources. Hall writes of 'the Queen, which entirely loved the Duke' and 'the Queen's darling, William Duke of Suffolk', and Holinshed incorporates the first of these phrases, but there is no evidence that they were lovers (*2 Henry VI*, ed. Warren, 29).

6. In his notes to this scene John Jowett attributes this point to Wolfgang Clemen's *Commentary on Shakespeare's 'Richard III'* (1957) (*Richard III*, 299). Clemen does not cite any English plays by way of parallel, but the patterned lament of the three Marys can be seen in the Chester Resurrection Play (Pageant 18).

7. To complicate matters further, Hall and Holinshed (following Hall) both wrongly call her Eleanor.

8. Shakespeare had already used a variant of these lines in *1 Henry VI*, when Suffolk, wooing Margaret on behalf of Henry VI (while in love with her himself), says: 'She's beautiful, and therefore to be wooed; | She is a woman, therefore to be won' (5.4.34–5).

9. Shakespeare here departs from the chronicles, which represent Elizabeth as persuaded by Richard and condemn her inconstancy. On this scene see further Jones, *Origins of Shakespeare*, 220–6.

10. See Christopher Marlowe, *Tamburlaine the Great*, ed. J. S. Cunningham and Eithne Henson (Manchester: Manchester University Press, 1998), 5.1.135–90.

11. There is good evidence that act and scene divisions were not generally used by Shakespeare but imposed on these plays after his death, in the First Folio. (While the choruses of *Henry V* do suggest that he conceived

of it in five parts, the Quarto text has no act divisions and the Folio act divisions do not correspond to the placing of the choruses.) The numbering of the scenes in the discussion above is not significant in itself except insofar as it is indicative of the rough point in the play where Shakespeare liked to introduce the private selves of some of his characters. On the question of act divisions see further Gary Taylor, 'The Structure of Performance: Act-Intervals in the London Theatres, 1576–1642', in Gary Taylor and John Jowett, *Shakespeare Reshaped, 1606–23* (Oxford: Clarendon Press, 1993), 3–50; Wilfred T. Jewkes, *Act Division in Elizabethan and Jacobean Plays, 1583–1616* (New York: AMS Press, 1972); and Emrys Jones, *Scenic Form in Shakespeare* (Oxford: Clarendon Press, 1971).

CHAPTER 7

1. *EEBO* records 'soloquie' [*sic*] in 1601 and 'soliloquie' in 1603, and in these and most other early occurrences the word is used in a religious context, to indicate a spiritual meditation. As Margreta de Grazia notes in her landmark essay on the nature of the early modern soliloquy, the English word 'derived from Augustine's coinage to describe a new and complex discourse: "I asked myself questions and I replied to myself, as if we were two, reason and I, whereas I was of course just one. As a result I called the work *Soliloquies*"' ('Soliloquies and Wages in the Age of Emergent Consciousness', *Textual Practice*, 9 (1995), 75). When a soliloquy is uttered in the theatre, however, the actor may choose whether to seem to be talking to himself, 'without addressing any person', or to be talking to the audience, and the very presence of an audience makes a real distinction between definition 1(a) and definition 1(b).

2. The choice of the male pronoun here is deliberate. There is almost no instance of a woman speaking in soliloquy in Shakespeare's English history plays. Margaret has a sequence of brief asides in *Richard III* (1.3.111–57) and speaks a few lines alone at the start of Act 4, scene 4 in the same play, before a further sequence of asides, but the effect is too passing to be compared with the other soliloquies examined here. Margaret is more than once scripted to speak at great length, but not to herself. Joan la Pucelle, in the scene where she summons the fiends to her (*1 Henry VI*, 5.3; see Chapter 8 below), also opens and closes the scene in speaking alone. *Macbeth*, Shakespeare's Scottish history play, shows Lady Macbeth in more extended soliloquy.

3. *Richard III*, ed. Jowett, 27.

4. The choruses in *Henry V* are present only in the Folio text, but this is generally agreed to have more authority than the Quarto text, and is thought to have been printed from an authorial draft.

5. *1 Henry VI* is associated with Lord Strange's Men, *2* and *3 Henry VI* and *Richard III* with Pembroke's Men, though, as Andrew Gurr notes, there is extensive reference to the Stanley family (of which Lord Strange was one) running through most of Shakespeare's plays written before 1594 (*The Shakespearian Playing Companies* (Oxford: Clarendon Press, 1996), 262). Some actors from Strange's, possibly including Shakespeare himself, moved to Pembroke's, and may have taken some plays and parts with them to the new company.

6. He also speaks aside once in *1 Henry VI*, at 3.1.61–4.

7. Antony Sher, *The Year of the King* (London: Methuen, 1990), 39.

8. On the text of this speech, see Chapter 3 n. 17 above.

9. *Richard II*, ed. Gurr, 2nd edn. (Cambridge: Cambridge University Press: 2003), 37.

10. Wells and Taylor, following the Folio text, print 'wise men ne'er wail their present woes' (3.2.174).

11. For further discussion of the case for regarding either sequence as planned see Nicholas Grene, *Shakespeare's Serial History Plays* (Cambridge: Cambridge University Press, 2002), chapter 1. Grene's own view is that 'the *Richard II–Henry V* plays are much less clearly written for serial production' than the *Henry VI–Richard III* series: 'in their formal distinctness and the weakness of the links between them, they [the *Richard II–Henry V* plays] suggest a set of individual compositions only incrementally accumulating into a series' (9).

12. *1 Henry IV*, ed. Bevington, 59.

13. *Shakespeare and the Dramaturgy of Power* (Princeton: Princeton University Press, 1989), 112.

14. On this characteristic combination of theatricality and opacity, see Cox, *Shakespeare and the Dramaturgy of Power*, 108–18.

CHAPTER 8

1. See, for example, the Bastard's speech in *King John* at 4.3.143–7 and 159, discussed in Chapter 7.

2. Bullough, *Narrative and Dramatic Sources*, iii. 402. On precedents and parallels for John of Gaunt's speech more specifically see Peter Ure's note in the Arden edition (p. 50).

3. Bullough, *Narrative and Dramatic Sources*, iii. 291.

4. *Hall's Chronicle*, ed. Henry Ellis (London: J. Johnson etc., 1809), p. 15.

5. Cf. here Alan Dessen's discussion of 'Theatrical *italics*' in *Recovering Shakespeare's Theatrical Vocabulary* (Cambridge: Cambridge University Press, 1995), chapter 5.

6. Grene, *Shakespeare's Serial History Plays*, 132 (citing Hall as above). Grene's chapter 5 provides a very illuminating discussion of curses and prophecies, in both the plays and the chronicles. Despite the presence of alternatives to the providential perspective in the chronicles, however, it is still the case, I think, that their set towards the material is less questioning than that of Shakespeare's history plays, where the very genre of drama, with its alternation of speakers and scenes, invites the routine construction of multiple perspectives.

7. How ghosts entered or exited is not always clear, but some scenes strongly suggest entry and exit through a trapdoor. The stage directions in Act 1, scene 4 of *2 Henry VI*, for example (further discussed below), indicate that the Spirit '*riseth*' and '*sinks down again*' (22 and 39). Bernard Beckerman, in a study of the plays performed at the Globe in the first decade of the seventeenth century, finds 'no evidence that the stage machinery was employed in the staging of ghost scenes at the Globe' (*Shakespeare at the Globe, 1599–1609* (New York: Macmillan, 1962), 203). He also notes in passing, however, that the use of the trapdoor is usually accompanied by thunder to mask the noise of the trap mechanism, and *2 Henry VI*, possibly first performed at the Theatre, does include thunder in the stage directions for the Spirit's entry and exit. Beckerman also suggests that there was 'no regular practice for costuming a ghost' (200), but it is clear from the evidence that ghosts are nevertheless often differently costumed from those around them. The pre-Globe play *A Warning for Fair Women* has a prologue that talks about ghosts being 'Lapped in some foul sheet, or a leather pilch [an outer garment made of animal skin]' (London: William Apsley, 1599, sig. A2^v, accessed via *EEBO*, 18 October 2010).

8. Both these scenes are Shakespeare's own additions to the chronicle sources (see also Chapter 3 above). The fact that Hall (and Holinshed, following Hall) report Richard's vision as a dream and do not implicate Richmond in any way makes absolutely clear that they do not accord the vision any otherworldly status, though Hall does also signal that he sees this stage of Richard's history as representing God's punishment (see p. 98 above), and Holinshed incorporates Hall on this point. Similarly, neither Hall nor Holinshed includes any independent endorsement of the appearance of fiends to Joan, though both report that she practised sorcery and witchcraft (Bullough, *Narrative and Dramatic Sources*, iii. 57, 61, 76–7). Hall especially dismisses her tales of 'visions, trances, and fables' as 'full of blasphemy, superstition and hypocrisy' and marvels 'that wise men did

believe her, and learned clerks would write such fantasies' (Bullough, *Narrative and Dramatic Sources*, iii. 57).

9. Again this scene greatly expands on brief hints in the chronicle sources. Hall notes that Eleanor 'by sorcery and enchantment intended to destroy the King' and records the names of those condemned with her for sorcery (Bullough, *Narrative and Dramatic Sources*, iii. 101). The more immediate sources of this scene, as Roger Warren discusses in more detail, are other plays, especially Marlowe's *Dr Faustus* and *Tamburlaine* (*2 Henry VI*, 82–3).

10. The word order allows a reading that makes the Duke the subject and Henry the object of 'depose', or the reverse of that; and 'him' is similarly ambiguous in its referent.

11. *The Statutes of the Realm (1225–1713)* (London: G. Eyre and A. Strahan, 1810–22), vol. iv, part i.

12. Reginald Scot's book *The Discovery of Witchcraft* (1584) is perhaps the best-known example of the emergent scepticism of the time. He argues very strongly that so-called witches are simply old women living alone and discredits many of the fraudulent practices masquerading as magic. On the general cultural shift from a belief in magic and witchcraft to a more rationalist stance, see Keith Thomas, *Religion and the Decline of Magic: Studies in Popular Beliefs in Sixteenth and Seventeenth Century England* (London: Weidenfeld and Nicolson, 1971).

13. The picture was first printed on the title page of the 1616 quarto.

14. A statute published in the fifth year of Elizabeth's reign notes the increase in the practice of 'feigning, imagining, inventing and publishing of such fond and fantastical prophecies, as well concerning the Queen's Majesty as divers honourable personages, gentlemen and others of this realm' since the expiry of the Edwardian statute against such practices with the accession of Mary I in 1553. It goes on to rule that anyone convicted of such prophesying with the intent to stir up rebellion shall be imprisoned for one year and, on a second offence, be imprisoned for life and forfeit all property. See Rupert Taylor, *The Political Prophecy in England* (New York: Columbia University Press, 1911), 105–7.

15. Bullough, *Narrative and Dramatic Sources*, iii. 195. Holinshed, as so often, is incorporating Hall word for word.

16. The transfer of monarchy from king to king usually passed from father to son, but Henry VI's son Edward is killed at the end of *3 Henry VI*. The Earl of Richmond, the future Henry VII, was a descendant of the same Lancastrian line as Henry VI. His mother, Margaret Beaufort, was the great-granddaughter of John of Gaunt, Duke of Lancaster. His marriage to Elizabeth of York, daughter of Edward IV, united the houses of Lancaster and York to form the new Tudor line.

17. In Holinshed Peter of Pomfret is not introduced until after Pandulph has taken and returned the crown to King John (having kept it for five days), and his prophecy is that John 'should be cast out of his kingdom' (Bullough, *Narrative and Dramatic Sources*, iv. 41). In *The Troublesome Reign of King John*, an anonymous two-part play to which Shakespeare was almost certainly also indebted, Peter predicts at the end of Part I that John will be dispossessed 'Of crown, estate, and royal dignity', but his prophecy is not recalled either when John hands over his crown or when it is returned to him (Bullough, *Narrative and Dramatic Sources*, iv. 116).

18. A further possible aspect of its mythologizing is its curious resemblance to Plato's account of the death of Socrates. See further Jones, *Origins of Shakespeare*, 20–1.

19. See the discussion in Chapter 5 (p. 65) and see further Dessen, *Recovering Shakespeare's Theatrical Vocabulary*, chapter 6.

20. Cf. e.g. *Pericles* (sc. 21.209–35), *Cymbeline* (5.5.122–216), *The Winter's Tale* (5.3.20–129), and *The Tempest* (5.1.58–142). E. E. Duncan-Jones identified a possible source for Katherine's vision in the funeral oration of Marguerite of Navarre (*Notes and Queries*, 206 (April 1961), 142–3), though it is not certain that Shakespeare or Fletcher knew this source.

CHAPTER 9

1. Both these plays, it should be noted, were collaborative.

2. Halio is following William Montgomery's edition of the play for the Oxford *Complete Works* (ed. Wells and Taylor). See Montgomery's note to this direction in *William Shakespeare: A Textual Companion*, ed. Stanley Wells and Gary Taylor with John Jowett and William Montgomery (Oxford: Clarendon Press, 1987), 619.

3. All stage directions from this point on will be quoted from the Folio, though line numbering will be in accordance with Halio's edition.

4. The word 'state', with the meaning either 'chair of state' or 'polity', occurs at least thirty times in *Henry VIII*. (The count is not exact, as the word can be used with the vaguer meaning of 'condition', and the word 'estate' can also be used in a way very close to 'state'.) Marvin Spevack's *Complete and Systematic Concordance to the Works of Shakespeare* lists twenty-two occurrences of the word 'state' for *Henry VIII*, excluding stage directions (Hildesheim: George Olms, 1968–94). No other history play comes close to this, and no other play by Shakespeare has more occurrences than *Henry VIII*, though *Coriolanus* has the same number in the text (again excluding stage directions).

5. Samuel Pepys was struck by this feature of the play, and found it the only enjoyable thing about it. '[T]hough I went with resolution to like it', he wrote, the play 'is so simple a thing, made up of a great many patches, that, besides the shows and processions in it, there is nothing in the world good or well done' (Diary entry for 1 January 1664, quoted in *Henry VIII*, ed. McMullan, 3).

6. See further Dillon, *Language of Space*, 107–16, where this scene and its relation to the historical sources are discussed in much greater detail.

7. The quotation is given in full in *King Henry VIII*, ed. McMullan, 59–60.

8. The Folio stage direction states that '*the King draws the curtain and sits reading pensively*' (61); but the fact that the King draws the curtain is to be understood as a stage necessity (to make him visible to the courtiers and the audience) rather than an indication of his intention to be made visible within the fiction. As his anger a few lines below demonstrates, he is observed unawares. As noted in Chapter 1 above, the use of the discovery space is rare in Shakespeare's history plays, though he uses it frequently in his other late plays. It is also just possible that a free-standing traverse (curtained enclosure) was used here instead of the discovery space.

9. Shakespeare is here following Holinshed, but Holinshed, following Stow, differs from the contemporary sources, which place the King below the Cardinals. (He too was on trial, since the trial was of the validity of the marriage itself, not of either party individually.) For fuller discussion of this point see Dillon, 'Trials of Queen Katherine'.

10. A few lines below Norfolk delivers an extremely detailed summary of his observation of Wolsey in this scene, extending over nine lines (112–20).

11. See e.g. 3.2.204 (stage direction), 5.1.88, 5.2.147 (stage direction).

Further Reading

Two very useful introductions to early theatre design are Andrew Gurr, *The Shakespearean Stage, 1574–1642*, 3rd edn. (Cambridge: Cambridge University Press, 1992) and Andrew Gurr and Mariko Ichikawa, *Staging in Shakespeare's Theatres* (Oxford: Oxford University Press, 2000). Good brief summaries of what is known about each of the early playhouses are to be found in Glynne Wickham, Herbert Berry, and William Ingram (eds.), *English Professional Theatre, 1530–1660* (Cambridge: Cambridge University Press, 2000). Scholarship on these playhouses continues to be updated, however, so numerous later publications contain revised information about the playhouses, especially those that it has been possible to excavate: the Rose and the Globe. See e.g. Julian Bowsher and Pat Miller, *The Rose and the Globe: Playhouses of Shakespeare's Bankside, Southwark: Excavations 1988–91* (London: Museum of London Archaeology, 2009).

There are several good general overviews of Shakespeare's history plays. Warren Chernaik's *Cambridge Introduction to Shakespeare's History Plays* (Cambridge: Cambridge University Press, 2007) is a good place to start, and volume ii of Richard Dutton and Jean Howard's *Companion to Shakespeare's Works* (Oxford: Blackwell, 2003) brings together a range of short introductory essays to the history plays. Paola Pugliatti's *Shakespeare the Historian* (New York: St Martin's Press, 1996) offers a useful synthesis and analysis of early modern historiography and critical approaches to the history plays, including a succinct account of the nature of Elizabethan historical writing. A clear narrative of the history of the period covered by Shakespeare's history plays, together with comparison of where Shakespeare deviates from history at key points, can be found in Peter Saccio's *Shakespeare's English Kings: History, Chronicle, and Drama* (Oxford: Oxford University Press, 1977). Most good editions of the plays will include relevant extracts from the chronicles in an appendix and discuss their relevance in the notes and introduction, but the sources for all Shakespeare's history plays are extracted and collected in volumes iii and iv of Geoffrey Bullough's *Narrative and Dramatic Sources of Shakespeare* (8 vols., London: Routledge and Kegan Paul, 1957–75). Annabel Patterson's ground-breaking study of Holinshed, *Reading Holinshed's Chronicles* (Chicago: University of Chicago Press, 1994), provides an important corrective to the view that the chronicle-writers were inherently conservative and spoke with one voice.

Two important predecessors of the approach taken here, focusing respectively on the nature of the scene and on the visual nature of Shakespeare's dramaturgy, are Emrys Jones, *Scenic Form in Shakespeare* (Oxford: Clarendon Press, 1971) and David Bevington, *Action is Eloquence: Shakespeare's Language of Gesture* (Cambridge, Mass.: Harvard University Press, 1984). Martha Fleischer's study *The Iconography of the English History Play* (Salzburg: Institut für Englische Sprache und Literatur, Universität Salzburg, 1974) also offers detailed analysis of the way stage images function iconographically in Shakespeare's plays. Alan Dessen has written pioneering books on the way visual signs operate conventionally on the early modern stage: *Elizabethan Stage Conventions and Modern Interpreters* (Cambridge: Cambridge University Press, 1984) and *Recovering Shakespeare's Theatrical Vocabulary* (Cambridge: Cambridge University Press, 1995). One of Dessen's articles, 'Stagecraft and Imagery in Shakespeare's *Henry VI*', *Yearbook of English Studies*, 23 (1993), 65–79, and a further article by Bruce Smith, 'Pageants into Play: Shakespeare's Three Perspectives on Idea and Image', in David M. Bergeron (ed.), *Pageantry in the Shakespearean Theater* (Athens, Ga.: University of Georgia Press, 1985), 220–46, also introduce vital concepts for understanding Shakespeare's dramaturgy briefly and very accessibly.

Further important studies in the field of Shakespeare's dramaturgy, including the extent to which he learned his dramatic art from medieval and Tudor plays, have been written by Robert Weimann (*Shakespeare and the Popular Tradition in the Theatre: Studies in the Social Dimension of Dramatic Form and Function* (Baltimore: Johns Hopkins University Press, 1978)), Barbara Mowat (*The Dramaturgy of Shakespeare's Romances* (Athens, Ga.: University of Georgia Press, 1976)), and Mark Rose (*Shakespearean Design* (Cambridge, Mass.: Belknap Press, 1972)), as well as again by Emrys Jones (*The Origins of Shakespeare* (Oxford: Clarendon Press, 1977)). Barbara Hodgdon's study of the endings of Shakespeare's history plays, *The End Crowns All: Closure and Contradiction in Shakespeare's History* (Princeton: Princeton University Press, 1991), also includes valuable analysis of his indebtedness to earlier theatre, and John Cox usefully highlights some of the differences between Shakespeare's plays and those of his predecessors in *Shakespeare and the Dramaturgy of Power* (Princeton: Princeton University Press, 1989). Brian Walsh's study *Shakespeare, the Queen's Men, and the Elizabethan Performance of History* (Cambridge: Cambridge University Press, 2009) provides an important context for Shakespeare's history plays by showing how much they are influenced by the plays of the Queen's Men, whose repertoire was strongly characterized by the earliest forays into the genre of the history play.

Other recent studies of the history plays worth following up are Phyllis Rackin's *Stages of History: Shakespeare's English Chronicles* (Ithaca, NY:

Cornell University Press, 1990); her feminist study of the histories, co-written with Jean Howard, *Engendering a Nation: A Feminist Account of Shakespeare's English Histories* (London: Routledge, 1997); and Nicholas Grene's study of the history plays as potential sequences, *Shakespeare's Serial History Plays* (Cambridge: Cambridge University Press, 2002). The 2010 issue of *Shakespeare Survey* (63), entitled *Shakespeare's Histories and their Afterlives*, brings together a number of interesting articles, including two useful general studies: Christy Desmet's 'Shakespeare the Historian' (1–11) and Jean-Christophe Mayer's 'The Decline of the Chronicle and Shakespeare's History Plays' (12–23). Desmet's essay examines changing emphases in secondary scholarship on the history plays, placing the work of such important earlier writers on the histories as E. M. W. Tillyard and Irving Ribner in the wider context of their times and looking too at more recent trends in analysis, including new historicism and biographies of Shakespeare. Mayer, as his title suggests, looks at the rise of the history play in relation to the decline of the chronicle.

Index